D0607347

QUESADILLAS

QUESA

DILLAS

DONNA KELLY

photographs by
SHEENA BATES

GIBBS SMITH
TO ENRICH AND INSPIRE HUMANKIND

With gratitude to my Southwest roots,
and to my mom, Carol Hicks, for raising me
to be strong, independent, and creative.

Second Edition
26 25 24 23 22   5 4 3 2 1

Text © 2010, 2022 Donna Kelly
Photographs © 2022 Sheena Bates
All rights reserved. No part of this book may be reproduced by any means whatsoever without written permission from the publisher, except brief portions quoted for purpose of review.

Published by
Gibbs Smith
P.O. Box 667
Layton, Utah 84041

1.800.835.4993 orders
www.gibbs-smith.com

Designed by Ryan Thomann
Printed and bound in China

Gibbs Smith books are printed on either recycled, 100% post-consumer waste, FSC-certified papers or on paper produced from sustainable PEFC-certified forest/controlled wood source. Learn more at www.pefc.org.

Library of Congress Cataloging-in-Publication Data
Names: Kelly, Donna, 1955– author. | Bates, Sheena, photographer.
Title: Quesadillas / Donna Kelly; photographs by Sheena Bates.
Description: Second edition. | Layton, Utah: Gibbs Smith, [2022] | Includes index. |
Identifiers: LCCN 2021031122 | ISBN 9781423660392 (hardcover) | ISBN 9781423660408 (epub)
Subjects: LCSH: Quesadillas. | LCGFT: Cookbooks.
Classification: LCC TX836 .K45 2022 | DDC 641.81/5—dc23

CONTENTS

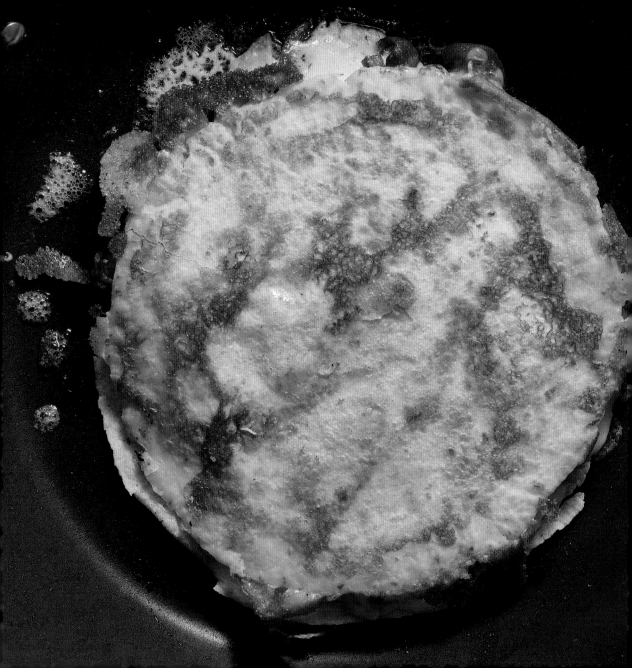

INTRODUCTION

QUESADILLA'S
ROOTS

SIMPLY PUT, the quesadilla is a delightful package of flavorful foods and melted cheesy goodness—all sandwiched inside crispy tortillas. It is the ultimate blend of Southwest old-world tradition and new-world foods. When the Spanish conquistadores arrived in Mexico in the fifteenth century, they found the natives eating what they described as "corn cakes." These were the ancestors of what we call "tortillas" today. The natives used tortillas like the Europeans used bread—as a side dish for their meals. They also used them as utensils, a sort of edible plate or spoon to hold other foods while eating. The Spaniards had enjoyed pastries stuffed with fillings and eaten like a sandwich, so the transition to using tortillas instead of pastry was an easy one. The word *quesadilla* loosely translates into English as "little cheese snack." Since the popular filling for these bundles is cheese, the term fits.

I grew up a few miles north of the Mexican border in Tucson, Arizona, where quesadillas were a staple in most households. They were a cinch for us kids to make—we just added a few handfuls of shredded cheese to a tortilla, folded it over, and cooked it in a skillet until the cheese melted and the tortilla browned. And, with the invention of microwave ovens, quesadilla time went from mere minutes to seconds. They were the perfect after-school snack food. The adults made fancier versions as appetizers for parties or with more fillings as a main dish.

Over the years, quesadillas have become increasingly popular all across America. The foods and spices of many diverse cultures are now often captured inside a quesadilla. The two essential ingredients are tortillas, which form the crisp outside crust, and cheese, which when melted is the necessary "glue" that holds the quesadilla together.

Quesadillas are so simple, delicious, and easy to make that their popularity has survived for centuries.

COOKING
TECHNIQUES

— — — — — — —

THERE ARE SEVERAL popular methods for making quesadillas. They can be baked, grilled, or cooked in a dry skillet. There are even specialty quesadilla makers available in the kitchen department of many stores. All methods use high heat to ensure the crispiness of the tortillas.

Baking
To bake quesadillas, simply put the stuffed tortillas on a wire rack on a baking sheet and place in the middle of the oven. Bake for about 20 minutes at 425 degrees. The actual baking time will vary according to how much filling is in each quesadilla. The more filling a quesadilla has, the longer it will take to bake. The goal is to have a quesadilla with the cheese fully melted, the filling heated through, and crispy tortillas. Watch closely the last few minutes of baking to make sure the tortillas don't become too brown. Nut- or cheese-crusted quesadillas require the baking method because the nuts and cheese

loosen and can fall off when turning the quesadillas in a skillet.

Grilling
For grilling, place the stuffed tortillas on a hot grill with very low flames, or place the quesadillas on the opposite side of the grill away from the flames. Close the cover and wait 1–2 minutes, watching closely so the tortillas don't become too brown. Carefully turn the quesadillas over with a very wide spatula, close the cover, and grill for another 1–2 minutes, or until the tortillas have browned and the filling is cooked through.

Toasting in a Skillet
The best method for cooking quesadillas is in a dry, covered skillet over medium heat, or in a quesadilla maker. When using a skillet, it should be dry, without oil or butter, in order to prevent oily or burned quesadillas. This toasting method also ensures that the filling will be cooked through, the cheese will be melted, and

the tortillas will be crisp and browned. I prefer making quesadillas with two flat tortillas rather than one folded tortilla because this ensures more even cooking. Choose a skillet that is just slightly larger than your tortillas. For example, I use a 10-inch skillet for tortillas that are 8-9 inches in diameter.

Start by placing a dry tortilla in a dry skillet that has been heated to medium heat. Place the filling ingredients on the tortilla, making sure that there is some cheese both underneath and on top of the filling. This will help the quesadilla stick together. Place another tortilla on top. Cover with a tight-fitting lid. This will hold in the heat and cook the quesadilla all the way through without burning the outside. Let the quesadilla cook for 1-2 minutes. Check to see if the bottom tortilla has browned. If so, carefully turn the quesadilla over with a very wide spatula. Cover and cook for another 1-2 minutes, or until the bottom tortilla has browned, the cheese has melted, and the filling is heated through.

INGREDIENT
TIPS

SINCE THERE ARE SO FEW ingredients in quesadillas, be sure to buy the best quality you can find. Ingredients must generally be cooked before being added to the quesadilla, because the purpose of the final cooking of the quesadilla is not to cook ingredients but to crisp the tortillas, melt the cheeses, and heat the filling through. Slice all ingredients thinly so that the quesadilla is relatively flat and has no large lumps or bulges.

Cheeses

Cheese comes in three general categories: melting cheeses, hard cheeses, and soft cheeses. Combining different cheeses in one quesadilla gives a greater richness than just one cheese.

In most quesadilla recipes, there is some type of cheese that melts well. This ensures that the quesadilla will be "glued" together. The most common cheeses for quesadillas are cheddar and Monterey Jack. Other types of cheeses

that melt well are fontina, Havarti, Gouda, Gruyère, and mozzarella.

Hard cheeses are primarily used for strong flavor. The most common hard cheeses are Parmesan, Asiago, and Romano.

Soft cheeses are also used for flavor and can be spread or crumbled. The most common soft cheeses are goat cheese, Brie, blue cheese, Gorgonzola, ricotta, Boursin, cream cheese, and mascarpone.

Tortillas

Flour tortillas are the best to use for making quesadillas. Corn tortillas can be used but generally do not become as crispy as flour tortillas when cooked

with the usual methods. Thinner tortillas are best, since the goal is to have a very crispy outside for the quesadillas. Try experimenting with flavored tortillas, such as those made with sun-dried tomatoes or basil. You may have to adjust the heat level or cooking time to make sure the flavored tortillas become crispy.

Filling Ingredients

The wonderful thing about quesadillas is that the only essential ingredients are tortillas and cheese, and any other foods can be used as fillings. For the most part, all ingredients should be thinly sliced and then cooked before being used as filling.

A good general rule is that 1 to 1 ½ cups of filling is the perfect amount for 8- to 10-inch tortillas. If you use more, the cooking time will have to be increased to allow the filling to heat through completely. Also, thicker quesadillas are trickier to eat, so you may have to use a fork and knife instead of your hands.

Since the cheeses mainly used in quesadillas are well salted, salt is not included as an ingredient in most of these recipes. Feel free to add salt and pepper to any of the savory recipes if you prefer your quesadillas on the salty side. The salt content of cheese varies according to brand and type, so taste the cheese first to determine saltiness.

Another wonderful thing about quesadillas is that they are a great vehicle for using leftover meats, vegetables, and cheeses. Yesterday's pot roast or other meat, thinly sliced or shredded, makes tasty quesadillas. They are a great way to clean out your fridge.

Since quesadillas have Southwest roots, try using spicy chiles with more mellow cheeses. Be adventurous, and you just might discover new food and flavor combinations that will surprise and delight you!

Sauces and Salsas

The last section of this book has recipes for delicious salsas and sauces to use with any quesadilla in this book—and those you may come up with in the future. Any quesadilla can be topped with any number of sauces or toppings, depending on your personal preference. Choose sauces that complement the quesadilla, such as Mushroom Cream Sauce (page 120) with the Mushroom Madness

quesadilla (page 90) or Roasted Red Pepper Sauce (page 119) with the Roasted Veggie and Goat Cheese quesadilla (page 78) or the Pecan-Crusted Pear quesadilla (page 116). The sweet or savory sauces are made to be drizzled over the top of the quesadillas just before serving or to be used as dipping sauces on the side.

Serving Quesadillas

Quesadillas should be cut into wedges with a pizza cutter to serve. They are made to be eaten with your hands. They can be served plain or with accompaniments. Popular traditional toppings include crumbled dry or grated cheese, melted cheese, sour cream, diced avocado, guacamole, diced onion, diced tomato or pico de gallo, and chopped fresh cilantro. Salsas and sauces can also be drizzled on top or used as a dip on the side. If you're having a quesadilla like Barbecue Chicken (page 23), try sprinkling cilantro on top and serving extra barbecue sauce on the side for dipping. Warm marinara sauce is delicious on the side of the Pizzadillas (page 33). Experiment with your own combinations—you will be surprised at how many work well together!

FAVORITES

WAFFLED
BREAKFAST

MAKES 4 SERVINGS

Wake up your taste buds with this breakfast quesadilla
cooked right in your waffle maker.

½ onion, diced

½ bell pepper,
any color, seeded
and diced

1 tablespoon
canola oil

½ teaspoon salt

½ cup diced cooked
ham, sausage, bacon,
or plant-based
meat substitute

4 large eggs

2 tablespoons milk

8 (6-inch) white
or whole-wheat
flour tortillas*

8 ounces pepper Jack
cheese, shredded

1. In a medium skillet over medium-high heat, sauté onion and bell pepper in oil for a few minutes, until slightly softened. Stir in salt and diced meat. Whisk together eggs and milk and pour into skillet. Cook, stirring, until eggs are cooked through.

2. Heat a waffle maker to high heat. Lay 1 tortilla in waffle maker. Sprinkle ¼ cup of cheese on top. Spread about ½ cup of skillet mixture on top. Sprinkle another ¼ cup of cheese on top. Lay 1 tortilla on top.

3. Close waffle maker top over quesadilla and let cook 1 minute. Press top of waffle maker down gently until quesadilla is flat and top of waffle maker covers all of top tortilla. Let cook a few minutes, until both top and bottom tortillas are golden brown. Repeat this process for remaining quesadillas. Serve immediately.

*Tortillas should be a bit smaller than surface of waffle maker. If tortillas are too large, cut to fit.

BACON JAM

The stunning flavor of bacon jam makes a heavenly breakfast quesadilla.

8 ounces bacon, finely diced

½ medium yellow onion, diced

1 medium shallot, diced

⅓ cup apple cider vinegar

¼ cup dark brown sugar

¼ cup maple syrup

8 (9- to 10-inch) white flour tortillas

4 ounces Monterey Jack cheese, shredded

1 Granny Smith apple, cored and shredded

1 ripe avocado, peeled, pitted, and diced

4 large eggs

1. Cook bacon in 10-inch skillet over medium heat until lightly browned, stirring frequently. Drain all but 1 tablespoon rendered fat out of skillet, reserving fat separately. Add onion and shallot to skillet and cook until very soft and browned, 3–5 minutes. Stir in vinegar and cook until very little liquid remains. Stir in brown sugar and maple syrup. Turn heat to medium-low and simmer until thickened, about 10 minutes. Pulse mixture in food processor into very small bits. Wipe out skillet with a paper towel. (NOTE: You will have leftover bacon jam. Refrigerate in an airtight container for up to 2 weeks.)

2. Lay 4 tortillas on a flat surface and divide ½ of cheese over each. Sprinkle ¼ of apple, ¼ of avocado, and 2 tablespoons bacon jam over cheese. Scatter remaining cheese on top.

3. Slide 1 covered tortilla into skillet over medium heat. Place 1 of the remaining tortillas on top. Press down with a wide spatula to remove any air pockets. Cover and cook 1–2 minutes, checking frequently, until bottom tortilla is crisp and browned.

4. Turn over, cover, and cook 1–2 minutes more, or until lightly browned. Repeat this process for remaining quesadillas.

5. Add 2 tablespoons reserved bacon fat to skillet. Turn heat to medium-high and cook eggs sunny-side up or to your liking. Top each quesadilla with an egg and drizzle more bacon jam on top. Serve immediately.

SMOKED **SALMON**

MAKES 4 TO 6 SERVINGS

Who needs a bagel with this crispy cheesy way
of eating smoked salmon?

8 ounces cream cheese, softened

8 (9- to 10-inch) white or whole-wheat flour tortillas

6 ounces fontina cheese, shredded

2 ounces Gruyère cheese, shredded

8 ounces Nova Scotia-style smoked salmon

½ cup chopped fresh dill

2 tablespoons drained capers, coarsely chopped

1. Spread 2 tablespoons cream cheese on each tortilla.

2. Toss fontina and Gruyère together in a bowl. Lay 4 tortillas on a flat surface and divide ½ of cheese mixture over each. Slice salmon into strips and place on top of cheese. Sprinkle 2 tablespoons dill and ½ tablespoon capers over salmon. Sprinkle remaining cheese over top.

3. Slide 1 covered tortilla into a 10-inch skillet over medium heat. Place 1 of the remaining tortillas on top, cream cheese side down. Press down with a wide spatula to remove any air pockets. Cover and cook 1–2 minutes, checking frequently, until bottom tortilla is crisp and browned.

4. Turn over, cover, and cook 1–2 minutes more, or until lightly browned. Repeat this process for remaining quesadillas. Cut into wedges and serve immediately.

THE CLASSIC

This classic quesadilla is a simple but sublime blend of cheeses and peppers.

3 large Anaheim peppers

6 ounces sharp cheddar cheese, shredded

6 ounces Monterey Jack cheese, shredded

3 ounces crumbled queso fresco

8 (9- to 10-inch) white or whole-wheat flour tortillas

1. Blacken skins of peppers by grilling, broiling, or using a kitchen torch. Place in a zip-top bag and seal. Allow to stand at room temperature for about 10 minutes. Take peppers from bag and remove skins by rubbing with a paper towel. Cut peppers open and remove seeds by scraping with a spoon; dice peppers.

2. Toss cheeses together in a bowl. Lay 4 tortillas on a flat surface and divide cheese over each. Sprinkle about ¼ cup diced peppers over top.

3. Slide 1 covered tortilla into a 10-inch skillet over medium heat. Place 1 of the remaining tortillas on top. Press down with a wide spatula to remove any air pockets. Cover and cook 1–2 minutes, checking frequently, until bottom tortilla is crisp and browned.

4. Turn over, cover, and cook 1–2 minutes more, or until lightly browned. Repeat this process for remaining quesadillas. Cut into wedges and serve immediately.

BARBECUE CHICKEN

The smoky taste of tangy chicken and Gouda make this
a must for your next backyard barbecue.

2 cups shredded
cooked chicken

⅓ cup barbecue sauce

½ cup minced
red onion

¼ cup minced
fresh cilantro

12 ounces smoked
Gouda cheese,
shredded

8 (9- to 10-inch) white
or whole-wheat
flour tortillas

Serving suggestions
Sour Cream-Paprika
Sauce (page 119)
or White Cheddar
Sauce (page 122)

1. In a bowl, toss chicken with barbecue sauce. In another bowl, toss onion, cilantro, and cheese together. Lay 4 tortillas on a flat surface and divide ½ of cheese mixture over each. Spread ½ cup chicken over cheese. Sprinkle remaining cheese mixture over top.

2. Slide 1 covered tortilla into a 10-inch skillet over medium heat. Place 1 of the remaining tortillas on top. Press down with a wide spatula to remove any air pockets. Cover and cook 1–2 minutes, checking frequently, until bottom tortilla is crisp and browned.

3. Turn over, cover, and cook 1–2 minutes more, or until lightly browned. Repeat this process for remaining quesadillas. Cut into wedges and serve immediately.

BLT

What a great Southwest twist on this classic sandwich favorite!

6 ounces fontina or Monterey Jack cheese, shredded

2 ounces sharp cheddar cheese, shredded

8 (9- to 10-inch) white, whole-wheat, or garlic flour tortillas

4 ripe tomatoes, seeded, diced, and drained

8 slices bacon, cooked and crumbled

4 cups shredded lettuce

2 tablespoons ranch or blue cheese dressing

1. Toss cheeses together in a bowl. Lay 4 tortillas on a flat surface and divide ½ of cheese over each. Sprinkle about ¼ cup tomatoes and ¼ cup bacon over cheese. Sprinkle remaining cheese over top.

2. Slide 1 covered tortilla into a 10-inch skillet over medium heat. Place 1 of the remaining tortillas on top. Press down with a wide spatula to remove any air pockets. Cover and cook 1-2 minutes, checking frequently, until bottom tortilla is crisp and browned.

3. Turn over, cover, and cook 1-2 minutes more, or until lightly browned. Repeat this process for remaining quesadillas. Toss lettuce in dressing and spread over top of quesadillas. Cut into wedges and serve immediately.

FAJITA STYLE

MAKES 4 TO 6 SERVINGS

This favorite restaurant dish makes mouthwateringly delicious quesadillas.

1 pound semi-frozen flank or top sirloin steak or frozen boneless, skinless chicken breasts

1 teaspoon lime zest

2 tablespoons lime juice

3 tablespoons canola oil, divided

1 tablespoon ground cumin

2 teaspoons chipotle chile powder

1 teaspoon salt

1 large yellow onion

2 bell peppers, any color

8 (9- to 10-inch) white or whole-wheat flour tortillas

8 ounces Monterey Jack or pepper Jack cheese, shredded

Serving suggestions
Sour Cream–Paprika Sauce (page 119), Creamy Avocado Sauce (page 121), or favorite salsa

1. Let meat stand at room temperature for 10–15 minutes. Thinly slice across grain and then place in a zip-top bag with lime zest and juice, 1 tablespoon oil, cumin, chile powder, and salt. Marinate at room temperature for 30 minutes, turning occasionally. Sauté meat in remaining 2 tablespoons oil in a large skillet over high heat for 5 minutes, stirring constantly, until browned. Remove meat from skillet.

2. Slice onion and peppers into ¼-inch strips. Add to skillet and sauté until softened and lightly browned. Stir meat back into skillet.

3. Lay 4 tortillas on a flat surface and divide ½ of cheese over each. Sprinkle about 1 cup meat mixture over cheese. Sprinkle remaining cheese over top.

4. Slide 1 covered tortilla into a separate 10-inch skillet over medium heat. Place 1 of the remaining tortillas on top. Press down with a wide spatula to remove any air pockets. Cover and cook 1–2 minutes, checking frequently, until bottom tortilla is crisp and browned.

5. Turn over, cover, and cook 1–2 minutes more, or until lightly browned. Repeat this process for remaining quesadillas. Cut into wedges and serve immediately.

TACODILLAS

Two classic beloved Mexican dishes melded into one.
Why haven't we thought of this before?

8 (6-inch) corn tortillas

2 cups shredded Monterey

8 ounces lean ground beef, turkey, or plant-based meat substitute

1 ½ teaspoons chili powder

1 ½ teaspoons ground cumin

1 teaspoon salt

2 tablespoons tomato paste

1 teaspoon cayenne pepper sauce

Salsa, diced tomatoes, shredded lettuce, grated cheese, or other taco toppings

1. Preheat oven to 350 degrees.

2. Spray 1 side of 1 tortilla with cooking oil spray. Place on a plate, oiled side down, and sprinkle with ¼ cup cheese, leaving about ½ inch around outer edge of tortilla bare. Place another tortilla on top, spray lightly with cooking oil spray. Repeat process 3 more times, making a total of 4 quesadillas. It's okay if they overlap slightly on plate. Microwave until just softened, about 30 seconds.

3. Place a small ball of crumpled aluminum foil on half of 1 quesadilla and fold other half over it, making sure foil creates a 1-inch gap in center of fold to create a taco shell shape. Place on a baking sheet. Repeat with remaining quesadillas to form 4 taco shells. Bake 25–30 minutes, turning shells over after 15 minutes, until lightly browned and crisp on both sides.

4. While shells are baking, cook ground meat, chili powder, cumin, salt, tomato paste, and pepper sauce in a 10-inch skillet over medium-high heat until meat is lightly browned. Remove from heat and keep warm.

5. Remove shells from oven and let cool slightly. Remove foil balls. Fill shells with skillet mixture and toppings as desired and serve immediately.

BUFFALO CHICKEN

MAKES 4 TO 6 SERVINGS

The marriage of this happy-hour classic and quesadillas is heavenly.

¼ cup Louisiana hot sauce or Tabasco sauce

2 tablespoons butter, melted

1 tablespoon apple cider vinegar

3 tablespoons brown sugar

½ teaspoon salt

2 cups shredded cooked chicken

8 (9- to 10-inch) white or whole-wheat flour tortillas

8 ounces sharp white cheddar cheese, shredded

1 cup very thinly sliced celery

½ cup thinly sliced green onions

Serving suggestions
Sour Cream–Paprika Sauce (page 119) or Creamy Avocado Sauce (page 121)

1. Preheat broiler with rack about 6 inches from heat source. Spray a baking sheet with cooking oil spray.

2. In a bowl, whisk together hot sauce, butter, vinegar, brown sugar, and salt. Add chicken and toss to coat. Spread chicken mixture on baking sheet and broil for 5–8 minutes, until lightly browned, watching closely so as not to burn. Turn chicken over with a wide spatula and broil for another 3 minutes.

3. Lay 4 tortillas on a flat surface and divide ½ of cheese over each. Spread chicken, celery, and green onions over cheese. Spread remaining cheese over top.

4. Slide 1 covered tortilla into a 10-inch skillet over medium heat. Place 1 of the remaining tortillas on top. Press down with a wide spatula to remove any air pockets. Cover and cook 1–2 minutes, checking frequently, until bottom tortilla is crisp and browned.

5. Turn over, cover, and cook 1–2 minutes more, or until lightly browned. Repeat this process for remaining quesadillas. Cut into wedges and serve immediately.

SHRIMP
ON THE BARBIE

MAKES 4 TO 6 SERVINGS

Grilled quesadillas on the barbecue are a favorite in the summertime—or anytime!

24 medium raw shrimp, peeled and deveined

¼ cup barbecue sauce

6 ounces fontina cheese, shredded

2 ounces Jarlsberg cheese, shredded

8 (9- to 10-inch) white or whole-wheat flour tortillas

1 (6-ounce) jar roasted red bell peppers, drained and diced

1 cup fresh or frozen and thawed corn

3 green onions, tops included, thinly sliced

Serving suggestions
Roasted Red Pepper Sauce (page 119) or Mushroom Cream Sauce (page 120)

1. Preheat a grill to high heat. Thread shrimp onto skewers and brush with a little barbecue sauce. Grill for 1–2 minutes on each side, or until just opaque and lightly browned. Remove from grill. Let shrimp cool, then slice in half lengthwise, creating 2 thin half-moons. Turn grill down to low heat.

2. Toss cheeses together in a bowl. Lay 4 tortillas on a flat surface and divide ½ of cheese over each. Spread a layer of shrimp over cheese, covering entire surface. Stir together peppers, corn, and green onions. Sprinkle ½ cup vegetables over top, followed by remaining cheese.

3. Place 1 of the remaining tortillas on top of each. Press down with a wide spatula to remove any air pockets. Place 1 quesadilla on grill, close cover, and cook 1–2 minutes, checking frequently, until bottom tortilla is crisp and browned.

4. Turn over, cover, and cook 1–2 minutes more, or until lightly browned. Repeat this process for remaining quesadillas. Cut into wedges and serve immediately.

PIZZADILLAS

MAKES 4 TO 6 SERVINGS

Everyone loves pizza—use these classic toppings,
or your favorites, for rave reviews!

8 (9- to 10-inch) white, whole-wheat, or garlic flour tortillas

6 ounces mozzarella cheese, shredded

1 cup marinara sauce

1 (6-ounce) can sliced black olives, drained

½ cup diced onion

½ cup diced green bell pepper

1 (8-ounce) package pepperoni slices, whole or diced

4 ounces Parmesan cheese, grated

1. Preheat oven to 400 degrees.

2. Place 1 tortilla in a 10-inch skillet over medium heat and sprinkle on ¼ of mozzarella cheese. Place 1 tortilla on top. Cover and cook 1-2 minutes, until bottom is lightly browned.

3. Turn over, cover, and cook 1-2 minutes more, or until lightly browned. Place on a baking sheet. Repeat with remaining tortillas and mozzarella cheese until you have 4 quesadillas on baking sheet. It is okay if they slightly overlap.

4. Spread ¼ cup marinara sauce on each quesadilla. Sprinkle a few black olives, 2 tablespoons onion, and 2 tablespoons bell pepper over marinara. Lay ¼ of pepperoni on top, covering entire surface. Sprinkle Parmesan cheese over top.

5. Bake 10-12 minutes, or until bubbly, checking frequently so as not to burn. Cut into wedges and serve immediately.

CROWD-PLEASER SHEET PAN

MAKES 12 TO 15 SERVINGS

This giant quesadilla is a crowd-pleaser—let your guests customize with their favorite toppings.

1 pound ground beef, chicken, or plant-based meat substitute

1 or 2 jalapeño peppers, thinly sliced (optional)

1 tablespoon ground cumin

1 tablespoon chili powder

1 teaspoon salt

1 tablespoon cayenne pepper sauce

2 tablespoons butter, melted, or canola oil

8 (9- to 10-inch) white or whole-wheat flour tortillas

8 ounces pepper Jack cheese, shredded

8 ounces sharp cheddar cheese, shredded

1 cup cooked black beans

1 cup corn kernels

Salsa, sour cream, sliced green onions, diced avocado, and sliced olives (optional toppings)

1. Cook ground meat in a large skillet over medium-high heat until lightly browned, breaking into small bits as it cooks. Add jalapeño (if using), cumin, chili powder, salt, and pepper sauce and cook another minute. Remove from heat.

2. Brush a 12 x 16-inch baking sheet with ½ of butter. Lay 2 tortillas on 1 long side, so that they are laying side by side and not overlapping, halfway on pan and halfway hanging off pan. Repeat on other long side. Place 1 tortilla on each short side, halfway on pan and halfway hanging off pan. Place 1 tortilla in center to cover any remaining bare pan.

3. Toss cheeses together in a bowl. Scatter ½ of cheese over tortillas. Spoon skillet mixture on top, spreading evenly over cheese. Scatter beans and corn evenly over meat mixture, then top with remaining cheese.

(continued)

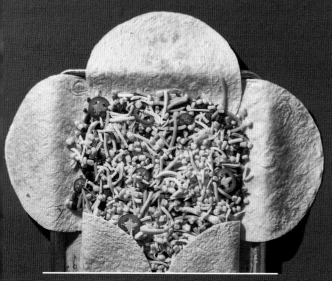

4. Fold overhanging tortillas up and over filling, flattening them on top. Place 1 tortilla in middle, covering any exposed filling. Brush all over top with remaining butter.

5. Place another baking sheet on top, pressing down to flatten quesadilla. Leave other baking sheet on top and place in oven. Bake 20–25 minutes, until tortillas are golden brown. Cut into squares and serve with toppings.

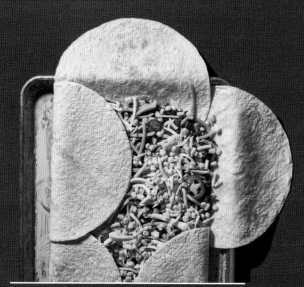

SEAFOOD MEDLEY

MAKES 4 TO 6 SERVINGS

The symphony of your favorite seafood will become
your own quesadilla classic!

1 pound assorted shelled raw seafood, diced (such as crab, shrimp, and scallops)

2 tablespoons butter

6 ounces fontina cheese, shredded

2 ounces Gruyère cheese, shredded

2 teaspoons Old Bay seasoning or other seafood seasoning blend

8 (9- to 10-inch) white or whole-wheat flour tortillas

1 cup chopped fresh parsley

1. Sauté seafood in butter in a skillet over medium-high heat until opaque and cooked through.

2. Toss cheeses and seasoning together in a bowl. Lay 4 tortillas on a flat surface and divide ½ of cheese over each. Sprinkle about ½ cup seafood and a little parsley over cheese. Sprinkle remaining cheese over top.

3. Slide 1 covered tortilla into a 10-inch skillet over medium heat. Place 1 of the remaining tortillas on top. Press down with a wide spatula to remove any air pockets. Cover and cook 1–2 minutes, checking frequently, until bottom tortilla is crisp and browned.

4. Turn over, cover, and cook 1–2 minutes more, or until lightly browned. Repeat this process for remaining quesadillas. Cut into wedges and serve immediately.

CALIFORNIA DREAMIN'

MAKES 4 TO 6 SERVINGS

Avocados are a natural addition to quesadillas and add a sweet, creamy goodness to this recipe.

2 large ripe avocados, peeled, pitted, and sliced

1 tablespoon lemon juice

½ cup mayonnaise

8 (9- to 10-inch) white, whole-wheat, or spinach flour tortillas

8 ounces pepper Jack cheese, shredded

8 slices bacon, cooked and crumbled

8 to 10 dried figs or apricots, finely diced

1 tablespoon smoked paprika

Serving suggestions
Roasted Red Pepper Sauce (page 119) or Creamy Avocado Sauce (page 121)

1. Toss avocado slices with lemon juice in a bowl.

2. Spread 1 tablespoon mayonnaise over 1 tortilla and place in a 10-inch skillet over medium-low heat, mayonnaise side down. Spread ¼ cup cheese and ¼ of bacon over top. Place ¼ of avocado slices evenly over bacon, followed by ¼ of dried fruit. Sprinkle another ¼ cup cheese over top and add a sprinkle of paprika.

3. Place 1 of the remaining tortillas on top and spread with 1 tablespoon mayonnaise. Press down with a wide spatula to remove any air pockets. Cover and cook 1–2 minutes, checking frequently, until bottom tortilla is crisp and golden brown.

4. Turn over, cover, and cook 1–2 minutes more, or until lightly browned. Repeat this process for remaining quesadillas. Cut into wedges and serve immediately.

NEW YORK DELI

East Coast flavors in a classic Western quesadilla!

¼ cup spicy brown mustard

8 ounces cream cheese, softened

8 (9- to 10-inch) white, whole-wheat, or spinach flour tortillas

8 ounces Swiss cheese, shredded

1 pound thinly sliced deli pastrami or corned beef

1 cup sauerkraut, drained

Serving suggestions
Sour Cream–Paprika Sauce (page 119) or Spicy Mustard Sauce (page 121)

1. Stir together mustard and cream cheese until smooth. Lay tortillas on a flat surface and spread mustard mixture over each.

2. On 4 tortillas, divide ½ cup of Swiss cheese over mustard mixture. Lay ¼ of pastrami over cheese, then sprinkle with ¼ cup sauerkraut. Sprinkle remaining Swiss cheese over top.

3. Slide 1 covered tortilla into a 10-inch skillet over medium heat. Place 1 of the remaining tortillas on top, mustard side down. Press down with a wide spatula to remove any air pockets. Cover and cook 1–2 minutes, checking frequently, until bottom tortilla is crisp and browned.

4. Turn over, cover, and cook 1–2 minutes more, or until lightly browned. Repeat this process for remaining quesadillas. Cut into wedges and serve immediately.

PHILLY CHEESESTEAK

MAKES 4 TO 6 SERVINGS

The traditional Philadelphia sandwich just went Southwest!

1 pound semi-frozen top sirloin or rib-eye steak

1 red bell pepper, seeded and sliced into thin strips

1 green bell pepper, seeded and sliced into thin strips

1 large Vidalia or yellow onion, sliced into thin strips

1 tablespoon canola oil

2 tablespoons Worcestershire or steak sauce

4 ounces provolone cheese, shredded

4 ounces Monterey Jack cheese, shredded

8 (9- to 10-inch) white, whole-wheat, or garlic flour tortillas

Serving suggestions
Spicy Mustard Sauce (page 121) or White Cheddar Sauce (page 122)

1. Let steak sit at room temperature for 10–15 minutes to slightly thaw. Slice across grain into paper-thin slices.

2. Sauté bell peppers and onion in oil in a large skillet over medium-high heat just until vegetables begin to soften, about 2 minutes. Turn heat to high and add steak. Stir and cook until lightly browned. Turn off heat and stir in Worcestershire sauce.

3. Toss cheeses together in a bowl. Lay 4 tortillas on a flat surface and divide ½ of cheese over each. Spread about 1 cup steak mixture over cheese and then remaining cheese over top.

4. Slide 1 covered tortilla into a 10-inch skillet over medium heat. Place 1 of the remaining tortillas on top. Press down with a wide spatula to remove any air pockets. Cover and cook 1–2 minutes, checking frequently, until bottom tortilla is crisp and browned.

5. Turn tortillas over, cover, and cook another 1–2 minutes, until bottom tortilla is crisp and browned. Repeat this process for remaining quesadillas. Cut into wedges and serve immediately.

TEX-MEX
CHILI CUPS

MAKES 4 SERVINGS

The cheesy goodness of quesadilla cups filled with
Tex-Mex chili will make your meal!

2 ounces sharp
cheddar cheese,
shredded

2 ounces Monterey
Jack cheese, shredded

8 (6-inch) white
or whole-wheat
flour tortillas

2 cups chili

4 tablespoons
sour cream

2 ounces crumbled
queso fresco

2 green onions,
with tops, thinly
sliced diagonally

1. Preheat oven to 375 degrees.

2. Toss cheeses together in a bowl. Lay 4 tortillas on a flat
surface and divide cheese mixture over each. Top each with
another tortilla. Place on a plate (overlapping slightly is fine)
and microwave for about 30 seconds, until tortillas are very soft.
Remove and press flat with a spatula.

3. Spray 4 (1-cup) ramekins or large muffin tins with cooking
oil spray. Place a softened quesadilla on top of each ramekin.
Using fingers, press quesadillas down into ramekins, making
sure bottom is pressed flat. Sides may be ruffled slightly to fit
inside ramekins. Spray with cooking oil spray. Place ramekins
on a baking sheet and bake 15–18 minutes, until quesadilla cups
are lightly browned and crisp. Remove from oven and let cool to
warm. If bottoms have puffed up during cooking, press flat with
a spoon.

4. Heat chili and ladle ½ cup into each quesadilla cup. Garnish
with 1 tablespoon sour cream, a sprinkle of queso fresco, and a
few green onions. Serve immediately.

SOUTHWEST LASAGNA

MAKES 6 TO 8 SERVINGS

Quesadillas make this Tex-Mex casserole a family favorite.

8 ounces lean ground beef, turkey, or plant-based meat substitute

1 ½ teaspoons chili powder

1 ½ teaspoons ground cumin

1 teaspoon salt

1 (6-ounce) can tomato paste, divided

4 ounces cheddar cheese, shredded

4 ounces pepper Jack cheese, shredded

5 (10-inch) white flour tortillas

1 (15-ounce) can red enchilada sauce

½ cup salsa

1 (15-ounce) can black beans, drained and rinsed

1 cup fresh or frozen corn

3 green onions, thinly sliced

1. Preheat oven to 350 degrees.

2. In a 10-inch skillet over medium-high heat, cook meat, chili powder, cumin, salt, and 2 tablespoons tomato paste until meat is cooked through. Empty skillet into a bowl and wipe out skillet with a paper towel.

3. Toss cheeses together in a bowl. Place 1 tortilla in skillet and sprinkle with ½ cup of cheese. Place another tortilla on top, cover, and cook 1–2 minutes, until lightly browned on bottom. Turn over, cover, and cook until lightly browned on bottom. Repeat to make a second quesadilla.

4. In a bowl, stir together remaining tomato paste, enchilada sauce, and salsa.

5. Spray a 10-inch springform pan with cooking oil spray. Place pan on a baking sheet. Layer ingredients as follows: 1 quesadilla, ½ skillet mixture, ½ black beans, ½ corn, ⅓ green onions, and ⅓ sauce. Repeat this process once.

6. Place remaining tortilla on top. Spread remaining sauce on top, then sprinkle with remaining cheese and green onions. Bake 25–30 minutes, until bubbly and heated through. Remove from oven and let cool a few minutes. Remove sides of springform pan and cut into wedges to serve. You can also make this recipe using a deep-dish pie plate and serve as a casserole.

SOUTHWEST DOGS

The classic American hot dog takes a Southwest spin in a crispy tortilla shell.

2 tablespoons cream cheese, softened

2 teaspoons yellow mustard

4 (6-inch) white or whole-wheat flour tortillas

1 cup shredded pepper Jack cheese

4 cooked hot dogs

Ketchup, mustard, or other dipping sauces

1. Stir together cream cheese and mustard. Lay tortillas on a flat surface and spread cream cheese mixture over each. Scatter ¼ of pepper Jack cheese over each tortilla. Place a hot dog at edge of each tortilla and tightly roll tortilla around hot dog.

2. Heat a 10-inch skillet over medium heat. Place wrapped hot dogs in dry skillet, seam side down. Cook until lightly browned on bottom, about 2 minutes. Turn about ¼ turn and cook for about 1 minute. Keep turning until all sides of tortillas are lightly browned.

3. Serve immediately with ketchup or other favorite dipping sauce.

TUNA MELT

MAKES 4 TO 6 SERVINGS

This cheesy tuna classic is a combination everyone will love!

1 (12-ounce) can solid albacore tuna, drained

2 stalks celery, minced

¼ cup minced red onion

¼ cup chopped fresh flat-leaf parsley

2 tablespoons chopped fresh dill

4 tablespoons cream cheese, softened

2 tablespoons lemon juice

1 teaspoon Dijon mustard

8 (9- to 10-inch) white or whole-wheat flour tortillas

8 ounces provolone cheese, thinly sliced

Serving suggestions
Creamy Avocado Sauce (page 121) or Spicy Mustard Sauce (page 121)

1. In a large bowl, mix together tuna, celery, onion, parsley, dill, cream cheese, lemon juice, and mustard.

2. Lay 4 tortillas on a flat surface and place a few slices of cheese on each, completely covering surface. Spread about ½ cup tuna mixture on top. Place a few more slices cheese over tuna, completely covering surface.

3. Slide 1 covered tortilla into a 10-inch skillet over medium heat. Place 1 of the remaining tortillas on top. Press down with a wide spatula to remove any air pockets. Cover and cook 1–2 minutes, checking frequently, until bottom tortilla is crisp and browned.

4. Turn over, cover, and cook 1–2 minutes more, or until lightly browned. Repeat this process for remaining quesadillas. Cut into wedges and serve immediately.

FOUR-LAYER FOLDED
RANCH

MAKES 4 SERVINGS

Chicken, bacon, and ranch dressing—what's not to love?

4 tablespoons cream cheese, softened

1 tablespoon dry ranch dressing mix

4 (8- to 10-inch) white flour tortillas

2 cups shredded cooked chicken

6 slices bacon, cooked and crumbled

4 ounces pepper Jack cheese, shredded

1. Mix cream cheese and ranch dressing mix together. Lay tortillas on a flat surface and spread cheese mixture over each.

2. Place a tortilla on a cutting board, and with tip of a knife at center of tortilla, cut from center out to edge of tortilla.

3. On first quarter of tortilla, next to cut, spread ½ cup of chicken. On next quarter of tortilla, sprinkle ¼ of bacon. On third quarter, spread ¼ of pepper Jack cheese. Leave fourth quarter empty.

4. Beginning at cut edge, fold empty quarter up over quarter with cheese, then fold again over quarter with bacon, and finally fold over quarter with chicken. You will have a 4-layer quesadilla in a wedge with bare tortilla on both top and bottom.

5. Heat a 10-inch skillet over medium-low heat and place folded quesadilla in skillet. Cover and cook about 2 minutes, watching closely until bottom side is golden brown. Turn over, cover, and cook another 2 minutes or so. Repeat this process to make 3 more quesadillas. Serve immediately.

TURKEY
CRANBERRY

Savor the traditional flavors of Thanksgiving dinner in a crispy tortilla.

8 ounces cream cheese, softened

3 tablespoons jellied cranberry sauce

8 (9- to 10-inch) white or whole-wheat flour tortillas

8 ounces smoked Gouda cheese, shredded

1 cup sweetened dried cranberries, chopped

½ cup chopped walnuts

1 pound deli turkey, sliced into 16 slices

1. Mix together cream cheese and cranberry sauce. Lay tortillas on a flat surface and spread cream cheese mixture over each.

2. On 4 tortillas, divide ½ of Gouda over cream cheese mixture, followed by 2 tablespoons cranberries, 1 tablespoon walnuts, and remaining Gouda. Place sliced turkey over cheese, covering entire surface.

3. Slide 1 covered tortilla into a 10-inch skillet over medium heat. Place 1 of the remaining tortillas on top, cream cheese side down. Press down with a wide spatula to remove any air pockets. Cover and cook 1–2 minutes, checking frequently, until bottom tortilla is crisp and browned.

4. Turn over, cover, and cook 1–2 minutes more, or until lightly browned. Repeat this process for remaining quesadillas. Cut into wedges and serve immediately.

INTERNATIONAL

OLD WORLD MEXICO

MAKES 4 TO 6 SERVINGS

This old-world combo of potatoes and chorizo is scrumptious with a touch of sweet or hot peppers.

8 ounces Mexican chorizo, casings removed, crumbled

1 tablespoon butter

1 large (12- to 16-ounce) russet potato, peeled and coarsely grated

3 cups shredded cheeses of choice, such as cheddar, Monterey Jack, Cotija cheese, or queso fresco

8 (9- to 10-inch) white, whole-wheat, or jalapeño flour tortillas

½ cup diced red bell pepper, jalapeño, or a combination of both

Serving suggestions
Sassy Smoky Salsa (page 118), Southwest Pesto Sauce (page 120), or Creamy Avocado Sauce (page 121)

1. Sauté chorizo in a 10-inch skillet until cooked through and lightly browned. Transfer chorizo to a plate and then add butter to skillet. Place grated potato in a kitchen towel and twist to wring out excess moisture. Sauté potato in butter until lightly browned, stirring constantly to remove moisture; remove from heat.

2. Toss cheeses together in a bowl. Lay 4 tortillas on a flat surface and divide ½ of cheese over each. Sprinkle about ⅓ cup chorizo, ½ cup potato, and 2 tablespoons bell pepper over cheese. Sprinkle remaining cheese over top.

3. Slide 1 covered tortilla into a 10-inch skillet over medium heat. Place 1 of the remaining tortillas on top. Press down with a wide spatula to remove any air pockets. Cover and cook 1–2 minutes, checking frequently, until bottom tortilla is crisp and browned.

4. Turn over, cover, and cook 1–2 minutes more, or until lightly browned. Repeat this process for remaining quesadillas. Cut into wedges and serve immediately.

THAI PEANUT

MAKES 4 TO 6 SERVINGS

Bold flavors from Thailand make this quesadilla exotic and flavorful.

1 (2-pound) rotisserie chicken

½ cup creamy peanut butter

2 tablespoons soy sauce

2 tablespoons lime juice

2 tablespoons grated fresh ginger

1 teaspoon Tabasco or cayenne pepper sauce

8 (9- to 10-inch) white or whole-wheat flour tortillas

8 ounces Monterey Jack cheese, shredded

½ cup thinly sliced green onions

½ cup chopped roasted salted peanuts

½ cup chopped fresh cilantro

1. Remove meat from chicken, cutting into small pieces as you go; discard skin and bones. In a bowl, mix together peanut butter, soy sauce, lime juice, ginger, and hot sauce. Stir in chicken and toss to coat.

2. Lay 4 tortillas on a flat surface and divide ½ of cheese over each. Spread about 1 cup chicken over cheese. Sprinkle some onions, peanuts, and cilantro over chicken, then top with remaining cheese.

3. Slide 1 covered tortilla into a 10-inch skillet over medium heat. Place 1 of the remaining tortillas on top. Press down with a wide spatula to remove any air pockets. Cover and cook 1–2 minutes, checking frequently, until bottom tortilla is crisp and browned.

4. Turn over, cover, and cook 1–2 minutes more, or until lightly browned. Repeat this process for remaining quesadillas. Cut into wedges and serve immediately.

FOUR-LAYER FOLDED CAPRESE

MAKES 4 SERVINGS

Take your taste buds on a European vacation
with this classic Italian combo!

4 tablespoons cream cheese, softened

4 (8- to 10-inch) white flour tortillas

1 (15-ounce) can diced tomatoes with garlic and herbs, well drained

4 ounces fresh mozzarella, thinly sliced

4 tablespoons basil pesto

1. Spread 1 tablespoon cream cheese on each tortilla.

2. Place 1 tortilla on a cutting board, and with tip of a knife at center of tortilla, cut from center out to edge of tortilla.

3. On first quarter of tortilla, next to cut, spread ¼ of tomatoes. On second quarter of tortilla, place ¼ of cheese slices, covering entire quarter of tortilla. On third quarter, spread 1 tablespoon pesto. Leave fourth quarter empty.

4. Beginning at cut edge, fold empty quarter up over quarter with pesto, then fold again over quarter with cheese, and finally fold over quarter with tomatoes. You will have a 4-layer quesadilla in a wedge with bare tortilla on both top and bottom.

5. Heat a 10-inch skillet over medium-low heat and place folded quesadilla in skillet. Cover and cook about 2 minutes, watching closely until bottom side is golden brown. Turn over, cover and cook another 2 minutes or so. Repeat this process to make 3 more quesadillas. Serve immediately.

HOISIN PORK
AND CABBAGE

MAKES 4 TO 6 SERVINGS

East meets West with these delightful and playful flavors.

4 cups thinly sliced bok choy

2 cups thinly sliced red cabbage

3 green onions, cut into 2-inch strips

2 tablespoons canola oil

¼ cup hoisin sauce

2 cups shredded cooked pork

8 (9- to 10-inch) white or whole-wheat flour tortillas

8 ounces Monterey Jack cheese, shredded

1 large egg mixed with 1 tablespoon water

½ cup sesame seeds

2 tablespoons olive oil or olive oil spray

1. Preheat oven to 400 degrees. Place a wire rack on a baking sheet.

2. Stir-fry bok choy, cabbage, and green onions in canola oil in a large skillet or wok over high heat for 3–5 minutes, or until softened slightly and most liquid has evaporated.

3. In a bowl, stir hoisin sauce into pork; set aside.

4. Lay 4 tortillas on a flat surface and divide ½ of cheese over each. Spread ¾ cup vegetable mixture over cheese. Sprinkle on ½ cup pork. Spread remaining cheese over top.

5. Place 1 of the remaining tortillas on top of each covered tortilla. Press down with a wide spatula to remove any air pockets. Brush tops of quesadillas with a little egg wash. Sprinkle on sesame seeds and brush or spray olive oil on top.

6. Place quesadillas, sesame seed side up, on prepared baking sheet. It is okay if they overlap, but you may need to bake in batches. Bake 10–12 minutes, checking frequently so as not to burn. Cut into wedges and serve immediately.

CARIBBEAN MOJO PORK

MAKES 4 TO 6 SERVINGS

Sweet mixed with spicy is a classic Caribbean combination—all stuffed in a quesadilla.

1 pound pork loin

Mojo Marinade (page 122), or use store-bought mojo marinade of choice

1 yellow bell pepper, seeded and cut into ¼-inch strips

1 red onion, sliced ¼ inch thick

1 large plantain, peeled and cut into ¼-inch slices

2 tablespoons canola oil

8 (9- to 10-inch) white or whole-wheat flour tortillas

8 ounces Monterey Jack cheese, shredded

1. Marinate pork in marinade in a large zip-top bag for 8 hours or overnight.

2. Preheat grill or broiler to high heat. Remove pork from marinade and grill or broil for 2–3 minutes per side, or until browned and crusty. Let cool to warm, then thinly slice.

3. Stir-fry bell pepper, onion, and plantain in oil in a large skillet or wok over high heat until lightly browned and softened.

4. Lay 4 tortillas on a flat surface and divide ½ of cheese over each. Spread 1 cup pork over cheese, followed by ½ cup sautéed vegetables. Sprinkle remaining cheese over top.

5. Slide 1 covered tortilla into a 10-inch skillet over medium heat. Place 1 of the remaining tortillas on top. Press down with a wide spatula to remove any air pockets. Cover and cook 1–2 minutes, checking frequently, until bottom tortilla is crisp and browned.

6. Turn over, cover, and cook 1–2 minutes more, or until lightly browned. Repeat this process for remaining quesadillas. Cut into wedges and serve immediately.

TANDOORI CHICKEN

MAKES 4 TO 6 SERVINGS

This Indian-inspired quesadilla takes the ho-hum out of dinner in a hurry.

½ cup plain yogurt

2 tablespoons lemon juice

2 tablespoons minced garlic

2 tablespoons minced fresh ginger

2 tablespoons brown sugar

1 tablespoon curry paste

1 tablespoon paprika

1 tablespoon ground cumin

1 teaspoon salt

1 teaspoon cayenne pepper

2 boneless, skinless chicken breasts

8 (9- to 10-inch) white flour tortillas

8 ounces Monterey Jack cheese, shredded

1 cup sliced toasted almonds

Serving suggestion
Peach Chutney
(page 123)

1. In a large zip-top bag, combine yogurt, lemon juice, garlic, ginger, brown sugar, curry paste, paprika, cumin, salt, and cayenne. Add chicken and refrigerate 2 hours or overnight.

2. Bring chicken to room temperature, about 30 minutes. Preheat a grill or broiler to high heat. Remove chicken from marinade and grill or broil for 8–10 minutes. Turn over and cook 5 minutes more, or until chicken is lightly browned and cooked through. Transfer to a cutting board and let stand 5 minutes, then thinly slice.

3. Lay 4 tortillas on a flat surface and divide ½ of cheese over each. Add ¼ cup sliced almonds, chicken slices, and remaining cheese.

4. Slide 1 covered tortilla into a 10-inch skillet over medium heat. Place 1 of the remaining tortillas on top. Press down with a wide spatula to remove any air pockets. Cover and cook 1–2 minutes, checking frequently, until bottom tortilla is crisp and browned.

5. Turn over, cover, and cook 1–2 minutes more, or until lightly browned. Repeat this process for remaining quesadillas. Cut into wedges and serve immediately.

ALOHA SHRIMP
AND PINEAPPLE

MAKES 4 TO 6 SERVINGS

Give your taste buds a trip to Polynesia with these fresh tropical flavors.

24 medium raw shrimp, peeled and deveined

2 tablespoons honey

1 tablespoon butter

1 cup thinly sliced 1-inch pieces fresh pineapple

8 (9- to 10-inch) white or whole-wheat flour tortillas

8 ounces fontina cheese, shredded

1 cup sweetened shredded coconut

Serving suggestions
Roasted Red Pepper Sauce (page 119) or Creamy Avocado Sauce (page 121)

1. Cut shrimp in half lengthwise, making 2 thin half-moons, then toss in honey until evenly coated. Heat a skillet or wok over medium-high heat. Add butter to skillet and then add shrimp. Stir and cook until shrimp are opaque. Transfer shrimp to plate.

2. Turn heat to high. Add pineapple to skillet, and cook stirring constantly and scraping up any browned bits. Cook until liquid has mostly evaporated, about 2-3 minutes.

3. Lay 4 tortillas on a flat surface and divide ½ of cheese over each. Top each with ½ cup shrimp, ¼ cup coconut, ¼ cup pineapple, and remaining cheese.

4. Slide 1 covered tortilla into a 10-inch skillet over medium heat. Place 1 of the remaining tortillas on top. Press down with a wide spatula to remove any air pockets. Cover and cook 1-2 minutes, checking frequently, until bottom tortilla is crisp and browned.

5. Turn over, cover, and cook 1-2 minutes more, or until lightly browned. Repeat this process for remaining quesadillas. Cut into wedges and serve immediately.

FOUR-LAYER FOLDED
CUBANO

MAKES 4 SERVINGS

The flavors of Havana are only minutes away!

4 tablespoons cream cheese, softened

1 tablespoon yellow mustard

4 (8- to 10-inch) white flour tortillas

1 (4-ounce) boneless pork chop, cooked and thinly sliced

4 (⅛-inch-thick) slices deli ham

1 large garlic kosher dill pickle, chopped

4 (⅛-inch-thick) slices Swiss cheese

1. Stir together cream cheese and mustard. Lay tortillas on a flat surface and spread cream cheese mixture over each.

2. Place 1 tortilla on a cutting board, and with tip of a knife at center of tortilla, cut from center out to edge of tortilla.

3. On first quarter of tortilla, next to cut, spread ¼ of pork slices. On second quarter of tortilla, place 1 ham slice, cutting to fit. On third quarter, sprinkle ¼ of dill pickle. On fourth quarter, place 1 cheese slice, cutting to fit.

4. Beginning at cut edge, fold quarter with cheese up over quarter with pickle, then fold again over quarter with ham, and finally fold over quarter with pork. You will have a 4-layer quesadilla in a wedge with bare tortilla on both top and bottom.

5. Heat a 10-inch skillet over medium-low heat and place folded quesadilla in skillet. Cover and cook about 2 minutes, watching closely until bottom side is golden brown. Turn over, cover, and cook another 2 minutes or so. Repeat this process to make 3 more quesadillas. Serve immediately.

SOUTH AMERICAN CHIMICHURRI

MAKES 4 TO 6 SERVINGS

Forget bottled steak sauce—this South American sauce pairs well with North American grilled steaks.

2 cups chopped fresh flat-leaf parsley

½ cup chopped fresh cilantro

½ cup extra virgin olive oil

3 cloves garlic, chopped

2 teaspoons red pepper flakes

2 tablespoons lime juice

2 tablespoons honey

½ teaspoon salt, plus more to taste

2 (8-ounce) sirloin or tenderloin steaks

Ground black pepper, to taste

8 (9- to 10-inch) white, whole-wheat, or jalapeño flour tortillas

8 ounces Monterey Jack cheese, shredded

1. In a food processor, blend parsley, cilantro, oil, garlic, red pepper flakes, lime juice, honey, and salt. Transfer ½ of sauce to a covered container and refrigerate until ready to serve. Pour remaining sauce into a large zip-top bag, add steaks, and refrigerate 2 hours or overnight.

2. Bring steaks to room temperature, about 30 minutes. Preheat a grill to high heat. Remove steaks from marinade and season with salt and pepper to taste. Grill until desired doneness, about 3 minutes on each side. Transfer to cutting board and let stand for 5 minutes, then cut across grain into ¼-inch-thick slices.

3. Lay 4 tortillas on a flat surface and divide ½ of cheese over each. Add steak slices, then top with remaining cheese.

4. Slide 1 covered tortilla into a 10-inch skillet over medium heat. Place 1 of the remaining tortillas on top. Press down with a wide spatula to remove any air pockets. Cover and cook 1–2 minutes, checking frequently, until bottom tortilla is crisp and browned.

5. Turn over, cover, and cook 1–2 minutes more, or until lightly browned. Repeat this process for remaining quesadillas. Cut into wedges, garnish with reserved chimichurri sauce, and serve immediately.

JAMAICAN JERK

MAKES 4 TO 6 SERVINGS

Fresh and spicy tastes of Jamaica shine in this flavor-packed quesadilla.

10 green onions, thinly sliced, divided

5 cloves garlic, peeled

1 Scotch bonnet or habanero chile, seeded

¾ cup ketchup

3 tablespoons soy sauce

1 lime, zested and juiced

2 tablespoons jerk spice blend, or more to taste

6 boneless, skinless chicken thighs

1 plantain, peeled and cut into ¼-inch slices

Canola oil, for brushing

8 (9- to 10-inch) white, whole-wheat, or chipotle flour tortillas

8 ounces smoked cheddar cheese, shredded

1 mango, peeled, pitted, and diced

1. Combine ½ of green onions, garlic, chile, ketchup, soy sauce, lime zest and juice, and jerk spice in a food processor. Process until smooth, then transfer to a large zip-top bag. Add chicken thighs and refrigerate at least 2 hours or overnight.

2. Bring thighs to room temperature, about 30 minutes. Preheat a grill or broiler to high heat. Remove chicken from marinade, reserving marinade, and grill or broil, basting with marinade, until cooked through. Transfer to a cutting board and let stand 5 minutes, then thinly slice. Place plantain slices on skewers, lightly brush with canola oil, and grill or broil for a few minutes until softened and lightly browned. Transfer to cutting board and chop.

3. Lay 4 tortillas on a flat surface and divide ½ of cheese over each. Add chicken slices, 2 tablespoons of remaining green onions, 1 tablespoon mango, plantains, and remaining cheese.

4. Slide 1 covered tortilla into a 10-inch skillet over medium heat. Place 1 of the remaining tortillas on top. Press down with a wide spatula to remove any air pockets. Cover and cook 1-2 minutes, checking frequently, until bottom tortilla is crisp and browned.

5. Turn over, cover, and cook 1-2 minutes more, or until lightly browned. Repeat this process for remaining quesadillas. Cut into wedges and serve immediately.

ALMOND-CRUSTED MOROCCAN

MAKES 4 TO 6 SERVINGS

Spiced chicken and dried apricots fill a unique almond-crusted quesadilla!

1 teaspoon almond extract

8 ounces cream cheese, softened

8 (9- to 10-inch) white or whole-wheat flour tortillas

2 ounces Gruyère cheese, shredded

1 (2-pound) rotisserie chicken

2 teaspoons ground cumin

½ teaspoon ground allspice

½ teaspoon smoked paprika

1 cup chopped dried apricots

1 large egg mixed with 1 tablespoon water

1 cup minced or ground almonds

2 tablespoons olive oil or olive oil spray

1. Preheat oven to 400 degrees. Place a wire rack on a baking sheet.

2. Mix almond extract with cream cheese. Lay tortillas on a flat surface and spread cream cheese mixture over each. Sprinkle ½ of Gruyère cheese over 4 tortillas.

3. Combine cumin, allspice, and paprika in a bowl. Remove meat from chicken, cutting into small pieces as you go; discard skin and bones. Add to bowl with spices and toss to coat. Spread 1 cup chicken on each tortilla with Gruyère cheese, covering whole surface. Sprinkle apricots on top.

4. Place 1 of the remaining tortillas on top of each covered tortilla, cream cheese side down. Press down with a wide spatula to remove any air pockets. Brush tops of quesadillas with a little egg wash. Spread ¼ cup almonds on top of each and press down with spatula, making sure almonds are pressed into tortilla. Brush or spray olive oil on top.

5. Place quesadillas, almond-crusted side up, on prepared baking sheet. It is okay if they overlap, but you may need to bake in batches. Bake 10–12 minutes, checking frequently so as not to burn. Cut into wedges and serve immediately.

GREEK
ISLES

MAKES 4 TO 6 SERVINGS

The salty goodness of classic Mediterranean ingredients is tasty in a quesadilla.

6 ounces feta cheese, crumbled

4 ounces Monterey Jack cheese, shredded

8 (9- to 10-inch) white, whole-wheat, or sun-dried tomato flour tortillas

1 tablespoon butter

3 cloves garlic, minced

1 pound frozen chopped spinach, thawed, drained, and pressed dry

½ cup pitted and minced kalamata or black olives

Serving suggestions
Roasted Red Pepper Sauce (page 119) or Mushroom Cream Sauce (page 120)

1. Toss cheeses together in a bowl. Lay 4 tortillas on a flat surface and divide ½ of cheese over each.

2. Heat a skillet over medium-high heat. Add butter and then garlic, stirring about 1 minute, or until garlic is fragrant. Add the spinach and cook, stirring constantly until most of moisture has evaporated, 3–5 minutes. Spread ½ cup spinach mixture and 2 tablespoons olives on each covered tortilla. Sprinkle remaining cheese over top.

3. Slide 1 covered tortilla into a 10-inch skillet over medium heat. Place 1 of the remaining tortillas on top. Press down with a wide spatula to remove any air pockets. Cover and cook 1–2 minutes, checking frequently, until bottom tortilla is crisp and browned.

4. Turn over, cover, and cook 1–2 minutes more, or until lightly browned. Repeat this process for remaining quesadillas. Cut into wedges and serve immediately.

VEGETARIAN

BLACK
AND BLUE

MAKES 4 TO 6 SERVINGS

You'll love this powerful combination of strong cheese and spicy beans.

2 (15-ounce) cans black beans, drained and rinsed

1 teaspoon Tabasco sauce

2 teaspoons ground cumin

2 ounces Monterey Jack cheese, shredded

8 ounces blue or Gorgonzola cheese, crumbled

8 (9- to 10-inch) white or whole-wheat flour tortillas

1 red bell pepper, seeded and diced

1. In a large bowl, mix beans with Tabasco sauce and cumin. Toss cheeses together in another bowl.

2. Lay 4 tortillas on a flat surface and divide ½ of cheese over each. Spread ½ cup bean mixture over cheese. Sprinkle about ¼ cup bell pepper over beans. Spread remaining cheese over top.

3. Slide 1 covered tortilla into a 10-inch skillet over medium heat. Place 1 of the remaining tortillas on top. Press down with a wide spatula to remove any air pockets. Cover and cook 1–2 minutes, checking frequently, until bottom tortilla is crisp and browned.

4. Turn over, cover, and cook 1–2 minutes more, or until lightly browned. Repeat this process for remaining quesadillas. Cut into wedges and serve immediately.

FOUR-LAYER FOLDED SMOKY
PORTOBELLO

MAKES 4 SERVINGS

The meatiness of the mushrooms and the sweetness of the
tomatoes make this a satisfying veggie delight.

1 (6-ounce) jar diced sun-dried tomatoes in oil

½ cup chopped yellow onion

3 cloves garlic, minced

1 large portobello mushroom cap, halved and thinly sliced

4 (9- to 10-inch) white, whole-wheat, or sun-dried tomato flour tortillas

4 tablespoons cream cheese, softened

4 ounces smoked Gouda cheese, shredded

¼ cup chopped fresh flat-leaf parsley

Serving suggestions
Roasted Red Pepper Sauce (page 119), Mushroom Cream Sauce (page 120), or Creamy Avocado Sauce (page 121)

1. Drain oil from jar of tomatoes into a large skillet over medium-high heat. Add onion and garlic and sauté about 2 minutes, or until fragrant. Add mushroom slices and cook until lightly browned and liquid has evaporated. Remove tomatoes from jar and dice.

2. Lay tortillas on a flat surface and spread cream cheese over each. Place 1 tortilla on a cutting board, and with tip of a knife at center of tortilla, cut from center out to edge of tortilla.

3. On first quarter of tortilla, next to cut, spread some tomatoes. On second quarter of tortilla, sprinkle ¼ of mushroom mixture. On third quarter, spread Gouda and parsley. Leave fourth quarter empty.

4. Beginning at cut edge, fold empty quarter up over quarter with Gouda and parsley, then fold again over quarter with mushrooms, and finally fold over quarter with tomatoes. You will have a 4-layer quesadilla in a wedge with bare tortilla on both top and bottom.

5. Heat a 10-inch skillet over medium-low heat and place folded quesadilla in skillet. Cover and cook about 2 minutes, watching closely until bottom side is golden brown. Turn over, cover, and cook another 2 minutes or so. Repeat process to make 3 more quesadillas. Serve immediately.

MANGO
BRIE

MAKES 4 TO 6 SERVINGS

The strong flavor of Brie is mellowed by the sweet
mango, with a little hot pepper added for zip.

8 (9- to 10-inch) white
or whole-wheat
flour tortillas

8 ounces Brie, warmed

2 ounces Monterey
Jack cheese, shredded

3 green onions with
tops, thinly sliced

1 small jalapeño
pepper, seeded
and minced

2 ripe mangoes,
peeled, pitted,
and thinly sliced

Serving suggestions
Sour Cream–Paprika
Sauce (page 119)
or Spicy Mustard
Sauce (page 121)

1. Lay tortillas on a flat surface and spread Brie over each.

2. On 4 tortillas, sprinkle Monterey Jack cheese over top,
followed by green onions and jalapeño. Layer mango slices over
top, completely covering surface.

3. Slide 1 covered tortilla into a 10-inch skillet over medium
heat. Place 1 of the remaining tortillas on top, Brie side down.
Press down with a wide spatula to remove any air pockets.
Cover and cook 1–2 minutes, checking frequently, until bottom
tortilla is crisp and browned.

4. Turn over, cover, and cook 1–2 minutes more, or until lightly
browned. Repeat this process for remaining quesadillas. Cut
into wedges and serve immediately.

SAUTÉED
GARLIC-SPINACH

Garlic and spinach sautéed together with a dash
of nutmeg is a delicious combination.

8 (9- to 10-inch)
white, whole-wheat,
garlic, or spinach
flour tortillas

8 ounces cream
cheese, softened

1 tablespoon butter

2 shallots, sliced

3 cloves garlic, minced

1 pound frozen
chopped spinach,
thawed, drained,
and pressed dry

½ teaspoon
ground nutmeg

2 ounces Gruyère
cheese, shredded

Salt and ground black
pepper, to taste

Serving suggestions
Sour Cream-Paprika
Sauce (page 119)
or White Cheddar
Sauce (page 122)

1. Lay tortillas on a flat surface and spread cream cheese over each.

2. Heat a skillet over medium-high heat. Add butter, shallots, and garlic and stir about 1 minute, or until garlic is fragrant. Add spinach and stir constantly until most of moisture has evaporated, 3-5 minutes. Remove from heat and stir in nutmeg.

3. Divide ½ of cheese over 4 tortillas, followed by ⅔ cup spinach and remaining cheese.

4. Slide 1 covered tortilla into a 10-inch skillet over medium heat and sprinkle with salt and pepper. Place 1 of the remaining tortillas on top, cream cheese side down. Press down with a wide spatula to remove any air pockets. Cover and cook 1-2 minutes, checking frequently, until bottom tortilla is crisp and browned.

5. Turn over, cover, and cook 1-2 minutes more, or until lightly browned. Repeat this process for remaining quesadillas. Cut into wedges and serve immediately.

ROASTED VEGGIE
AND GOAT CHEESE

MAKES 4 TO 6 SERVINGS

This combination of roasted veggies and goat cheese is simply delightful.

1 large yellow onion, cut into 1-inch strips

2 red bell peppers, seeded and cut into 1-inch strips

1 large bunch asparagus, trimmed and cut into 1-inch strips

3 small zucchini, cut into 1-inch strips

3 tablespoons olive oil, divided

5 cloves garlic, minced

8 (9- to 10-inch) white, whole-wheat, or pesto flour tortillas

8 ounces goat cheese, softened

1 teaspoon salt

Serving suggestions
Roasted Red Pepper Sauce (page 119) or Mushroom Cream Sauce (page 120)

1. Preheat oven to 425 degrees.

2. Place onion, bell peppers, asparagus, and zucchini, cut side down, in a baking pan and brush with 2 tablespoons oil. Bake 15 minutes. Remove from oven, and sprinkle with garlic. Return to oven for 12-15 minutes more, or until vegetables are softened and lightly browned.

3. Lay tortillas on a flat surface and spread goat cheese over each, then sprinkle salt on top.

4. Heat a 10-inch skillet over medium heat. Slide 1 covered tortilla into skillet. Spread 1 cup roasted vegetable mixture over top. Place 1 of the remaining tortillas on top, goat-cheese side down. Press down with a wide spatula to remove any air pockets. Cover and cook 1-2 minutes, checking frequently, until bottom tortilla is crisp and browned.

5. Turn over, cover, and cook 1-2 minutes more, or until lightly browned. Repeat this process for remaining quesadillas. Cut into wedges and serve immediately.

VEGAN CASHEW CREAM

MAKES 4 SERVINGS

You won't miss the dairy in this flavorful plant-based quesadilla with a smoky chipotle kick.

1 cup roasted cashews

1 canned chipotle pepper in adobo sauce

Salt and ground black pepper, to taste

2 tablespoons coconut oil

½ red bell pepper, sliced into ¼-inch strips

½ yellow onion, sliced into ¼-inch strips

1 large portobello mushroom cap, sliced into ¼-inch slices

3 green onions, thinly sliced

8 (9- to 10-inch) white flour tortillas

1. Put cashews in a heatproof bowl or saucepan, cover with boiling water, and let sit about 30 minutes, or until mushy. Drain cashews, reserving liquid. In a blender, blend cashews, chipotle pepper, and a little salt and pepper until very smooth. Add reserved liquid, 1 tablespoon at a time, to reach consistency of nut butter.

2. In a 10-inch skillet, add coconut oil and then cook bell pepper and onion quickly over high heat about 1 minute, stirring constantly. Add mushroom to skillet and sprinkle with a little salt and pepper. Sauté another minute or so, until all vegetables are softened slightly. Add a little salt and pepper to taste. Remove from heat and stir in green onions.

3. Lay tortillas on a flat surface and spread a thin layer of cashew cream over each.

4. Slide 1 covered tortilla into a 10-inch skillet over medium heat. Sprinkle with about 1 cup sautéed vegetables. Place 1 of the remaining tortillas, cream side down, on top. Press down with a wide spatula to remove any air pockets. Cover and cook about 1–2 minutes, checking frequently until bottom tortilla is crisp and browned.

5. Turn over, cover, and cook 1–2 minutes more, or until lightly browned. Repeat this process for remaining quesadillas. Cut into wedges and serve immediately.

BUTTERNUT SQUASH

MAKES 4 TO 6 SERVINGS

The soft texture of the squash and cheese combined with the crunchiness of the pecans is delightful.

1 butternut squash, peeled, cut in half lengthwise, and seeds and strings removed

2 tablespoons butter

1 tablespoon brown sugar

1 large white or yellow onion, cut in half and then into ¼-inch slices

8 (9- to 10-inch) white or whole-wheat flour tortillas

8 ounces fontina cheese, shredded

1 cup chopped pecans

Serving suggestions
Roasted Red Pepper Sauce (page 119) or Mushroom Cream Sauce (page 120)

1. Preheat oven to 375 degrees. Spray a baking sheet with cooking oil spray.

2. Place squash halves, cut side down, on prepared baking sheet and bake 40–50 minutes, or until fork-tender. Cool and cut into ¼-inch slices.

3. Heat a skillet over medium-high heat. Add butter, brown sugar, and onion. Cook, stirring occasionally, until caramelized, about 15 minutes.

4. Lay 4 tortillas on a flat surface and divide ½ of cheese over each. Top with ½ cup squash, ¼ cup onion, ¼ cup pecans, and remaining cheese.

5. Slide 1 covered tortilla into a 10-inch skillet over medium heat. Place 1 of the remaining tortillas on top. Press down with a wide spatula to remove any air pockets. Cover and cook 1–2 minutes, checking frequently, until bottom tortilla is crisp and browned.

6. Turn over, cover, and cook 1–2 minutes more, or until lightly browned. Repeat this process for remaining quesadillas. Cut into wedges and serve immediately.

ROASTED GARLIC

MAKES 4 TO 6 SERVINGS

If you're a garlic lover, put this on your top-ten list for favorite garlic recipes!

2 bulbs elephant garlic or 3 bulbs regular garlic

2 tablespoons olive oil

Salt and ground black pepper, to taste

2 ounces Monterey Jack cheese, shredded

6 ounces feta cheese, crumbled

8 (9- to 10-inch) white, whole-wheat, or garlic flour tortillas

2 green onions, thinly sliced

1 cup toasted sliced almonds

Serving suggestions
Roasted Red Pepper Sauce (page 119) or Mushroom Cream Sauce (page 120)

1. Preheat oven to 350 degrees.

2. Slice garlic bulbs in half (across diameter) and place, cut side up, on a sheet of aluminum foil. Drizzle with oil and fold foil up around garlic bulbs to enclose. Bake 1 hour, then let cool. Squeeze garlic cloves from skins and mash with a fork until creamy. Add salt and pepper.

3. Toss cheeses together in a bowl. Lay tortillas on a flat surface and spread garlic over each. Divide ½ of cheese over 4 tortillas. Top with green onions, almonds, and remaining cheese.

4. Slide 1 covered tortilla into a 10-inch skillet over medium heat. Place 1 of the remaining tortillas, garlic side down, on top. Press down with a wide spatula to remove any air pockets. Cover and cook about 1–2 minutes, checking frequently until bottom tortilla is crisp and browned.

5. Turn over, cover, and cook 1–2 minutes more, or until lightly browned. Repeat this process for remaining quesadillas. Cut into wedges and serve immediately.

THREE-BEAN TORTE

You won't miss the meat with this hearty cheese torte.

2 (14-ounce) cans black beans, drained and rinsed

1 (14-ounce) can pinto beans, drained and rinsed

1 (14-ounce) can white beans, drained and rinsed

1 (10-ounce) can red enchilada sauce

1 cup salsa

4 ounces Monterey Jack cheese, shredded, plus more for optional garnish

8 ounces cheddar cheese, shredded

8 (9- to 10-inch) white, whole-wheat, or jalapeño flour tortillas

2 cups fresh or frozen and thawed corn

½ cup chopped fresh cilantro

1 cup thinly sliced green onions

1. Preheat oven to 350 degrees.

2. Stir together beans in a large bowl. Stir together enchilada sauce and salsa in a separate bowl. Mix cheeses in a third bowl.

3. Spray a 10-inch springform pan with cooking oil spray. Put 1 tortilla in prepared pan, then add a little corn, cilantro, sauce, beans, green onions, and cheese. Repeat to make 6 more layers, then top with last tortilla.

4. Bake 30–40 minutes, or until bubbly and cooked throughout. Remove from oven and let stand 5 minutes. Remove sides of springform pan and garnish torte with a little more shredded cheese, if desired. Cut into wedges and serve immediately. You can also make this recipe using a deep-dish pie plate and serve as a casserole.

SPRING FLING

The fresh flavors of spring vegetables are scrumptious
with your favorite melted cheese.

1 bunch thin
asparagus,
trimmed and cut
into 2-inch pieces

2 cups tiny grape
tomatoes

1 bunch green onions
with tops, thinly sliced

3 cloves garlic, minced

2 tablespoons olive oil

Salt and ground black
pepper, to taste

8 (9- to 10-inch) white,
whole-wheat, or
spinach flour tortillas

8 ounces fontina
cheese or other mild
cheese, shredded

Serving suggestions
Mushroom Cream
Sauce (page 120)
or White Cheddar
Sauce (page 122)

1. Preheat broiler with rack about 6 inches from heat source. Spray a rimmed baking sheet with cooking oil spray.

2. Spread asparagus, tomatoes, green onions, and garlic on prepared sheet. Brush vegetables with olive oil. Broil for 3-5 minutes, watching closely, until vegetables are cooked and lightly browned. Remove from oven and sprinkle with salt and pepper.

3. Lay 4 tortillas on a flat surface and divide ½ of cheese over each. Spread about 1 cup vegetables over cheese. Sprinkle remaining cheese over top.

4. Slide 1 covered tortilla into a 10-inch skillet over medium heat. Place 1 of the remaining tortillas on top. Press down with a wide spatula to remove any air pockets. Cover and cook 1-2 minutes, checking frequently, until bottom tortilla is crisp and browned.

5. Turn over, cover, and cook 1-2 minutes more, or until lightly browned. Repeat this process for remaining quesadillas. Cut into wedges and serve immediately.

THREE-CHEESE BROCCOLI

MAKES 4 TO 6 SERVINGS

The favorite combo of broccoli and cheese is extra tasty in a cheddar-crusted quesadilla.

2 tablespoons butter

4 cups chopped broccoli florets

½ cup chopped onion

6 ounces sharp cheddar cheese, shredded

2 ounces Gruyère cheese, shredded

2 ounces Parmesan cheese, shredded

8 (9- to 10-inch) white or whole-wheat flour tortillas

Serving suggestions
Spicy Mustard Sauce (page 121) or White Cheddar Sauce (page 122)

1. Preheat oven to 400 degrees. Place a wire rack on a baking sheet.

2. Heat a large skillet over medium-high heat. Add butter, broccoli, and onion. Sauté for 3–5 minutes, or until broccoli and onion are softened and most of liquid has evaporated.

3. Put 1 cup of cheddar cheese in a bowl and set aside. In another bowl, toss Gruyère, Parmesan, and remaining cheddar together. Lay 4 tortillas on a flat surface and divide ½ of cheese mixture over each. Sprinkle broccoli mixture over cheese. Sprinkle remaining cheese mixture over top.

4. Place 1 of the remaining tortillas on top of each. Press down with a wide spatula to remove any air pockets. Brush tops of quesadillas with a little water. Divide reserved 1 cup cheddar cheese on top in an even layer.

5. Place quesadillas, cheddar cheese side up, on prepared baking sheet. It is okay if they overlap, but you may need to bake in batches. Bake 10–12 minutes, checking frequently so as not to burn. Cut into wedges and serve immediately.

MUSHROOM MADNESS

MAKES 4 TO 6 SERVINGS

If you love mushrooms, put this flavorful recipe on your must-try list.

3 tablespoons butter, divided

12 cups thinly sliced mushrooms, any combination such as portobello, cremini, and shiitake

3 cloves garlic, minced

½ cup thinly sliced green onions

8 (9- to 10-inch) white, whole-wheat, or garlic flour tortillas

8 ounces regular or smoked Gouda cheese, shredded

Serving suggestions

Mushroom Cream Sauce (page 120) or Spicy Mustard Sauce (page 121)

1. Melt 1 ½ tablespoons butter in a 10-inch skillet over medium-high heat. Add ½ of mushrooms and ½ of garlic and sauté until most of moisture has evaporated and mushrooms are lightly browned. Transfer mushrooms to bowl and repeat with remaining butter, mushrooms, and garlic. Add mushrooms to bowl and stir in green onions.

2. Lay 4 tortillas on a flat surface and divide ½ of cheese over each. Spread 1 cup mushrooms over cheese. Sprinkle remaining cheese over top.

3. Slide 1 covered tortilla into a 10-inch skillet over medium heat. Place 1 of the remaining tortillas on top. Press down with a wide spatula to remove any air pockets. Cover and cook 1–2 minutes, checking frequently, until bottom tortilla is crisp and browned.

4. Turn over, cover, and cook 1–2 minutes more, or until lightly browned. Repeat this process for remaining quesadillas. Cut into wedges and serve immediately.

CARAMELIZED ONION GOUDA

MAKES 4 TO 6 SERVINGS

Sweet caramelized onions are the perfect flavor match for smoky Gouda.

2 medium white onions, cut into ¼-inch slices

2 tablespoons butter

1 tablespoon brown sugar

1 teaspoon white wine vinegar

½ teaspoon salt

8 (9- to 10-inch) white or whole-wheat flour tortillas

8 ounces smoked Gouda cheese, shredded

1 cup chopped fresh flat-leaf parsley

Serving suggestions

Mushroom Cream Sauce (page 120) or Creamy Avocado Sauce (page 121)

1. In a 10-inch skillet, sauté onions in butter, stirring constantly, for 15 minutes over medium-high heat. Add brown sugar, vinegar, and salt and continue to sauté until most of moisture has evaporated and onions are browned but not mushy.

2. Lay 4 tortillas on a flat surface and divide ½ of cheese over each. Spread ½ cup onion mixture over cheese. Sprinkle a little parsley and remaining cheese over top.

3. Slide 1 covered tortilla into a 10-inch skillet over medium heat. Place 1 of the remaining tortillas on top. Press down with a wide spatula to remove any air pockets. Cover and cook 1-2 minutes, checking frequently, until bottom tortilla is crisp and browned.

4. Turn over, cover, and cook 1-2 minutes more, or until lightly browned. Repeat for remaining quesadillas. Cut into wedges and serve immediately.

FOUR-LAYER FOLDED CONFETTI

MAKES 4 SERVINGS

The browned and roasted corn adds great flavor to the other crunchy vegetables.

2 cups fresh or frozen and thawed corn

1 tablespoon butter

½ red bell pepper, chopped

½ green bell pepper, chopped

½ red onion, chopped

4 (9- to 10-inch) white, whole-wheat, or chipotle flour tortillas

4 tablespoons cream cheese, softened

8 ounces Monterey Jack cheese, shredded

¼ cup chopped fresh cilantro

Serving suggestions
Roasted Red Pepper Sauce (page 119) or White Cheddar Sauce (page 122)

1. Heat a 10-inch skillet over medium-high heat. Add corn to dry skillet and cook 5–8 minutes, stirring constantly, until corn is lightly browned. Transfer corn to bowl. Add butter and bell peppers to skillet and sauté until slightly softened. Transfer to separate bowl. Add onion to skillet and sauté until slightly softened. Transfer to third bowl.

2. Lay tortillas on a flat surface and spread cream cheese over each.

3. Place 1 tortilla on a cutting board, and with tip of a knife at center of tortilla, cut from center out to edge of tortilla.

4. On first quarter of tortilla, next to cut, sprinkle ¼ of corn. On second quarter of tortilla, sprinkle ¼ of peppers. On third quarter, spread ¼ of onion. On fourth quarter, spread ¼ of cheese and cilantro.

5. Beginning at cut edge, fold quarter with cheese up over quarter with onion, then fold again over quarter with peppers, and finally fold over quarter with corn. You will have a 4-layer quesadilla in a wedge with bare tortilla on both top and bottom.

6. Heat a 10-inch skillet over medium-low heat and place folded quesadilla in skillet. Cover and cook about 2 minutes, watching closely until bottom side is golden brown. Turn over, cover, and cook another 2 minutes or so. Repeat process to make 3 more quesadillas. Serve immediately.

ROASTED RATATOUILLE

MAKES 4 TO 6 SERVINGS

The classic combination of roasted eggplant, squash, and onions makes delectable quesadillas.

1 large yellow onion

3 small yellow squash

3 small zucchini

1 medium eggplant

2 tablespoons olive oil

2 teaspoons garlic powder

8 (9- to 10-inch) white, whole-wheat, or garlic flour tortillas

8 ounces Jarlsberg or Gruyère cheese, shredded

Serving suggestions
Roasted Red Pepper Sauce (page 119) or Mushroom Cream Sauce (page 120)

1. Preheat broiler with rack about 6 inches from heat source.

2. Slice onion, squash, zucchini, and eggplant lengthwise into ¼-inch-thick planks. Cut planks into 2-inch-long strips. Place vegetables close together, cut side down, in a baking pan and brush with oil. Sprinkle with garlic powder. Broil for 3–5 minutes, or until lightly browned. Remove from oven and let cool.

3. Lay 4 tortillas on a flat surface and divide ½ of cheese over each. Spread about 1 cup vegetables over cheese and top with remaining cheese.

4. Slide 1 covered tortilla into a 10-inch skillet over medium heat. Place 1 of the remaining tortillas on top. Press down with a wide spatula to remove any air pockets. Cover and cook 1–2 minutes, checking frequently, until bottom tortilla is crisp and browned.

5. Turn over, cover, and cook 1–2 minutes more, or until lightly browned. Repeat for remaining quesadillas. Cut into wedges and serve immediately.

THREE-OLIVE

If you love strong, exotic flavors, this is the quesadilla for you.

2 ounces Gruyère cheese, shredded

6 ounces fontina cheese, shredded

4 ounces stuffed green olives, thinly sliced

4 ounces pitted kalamata olives, thinly sliced

8 ounces pitted black olives, thinly sliced

½ cup chopped fresh flat-leaf parsley

8 (9- to 10-inch) white or whole-wheat flour tortillas

Serving suggestions
Creamy Avocado Sauce (page 121) or White Cheddar Sauce (page 122)

1. Toss cheeses together in a bowl. Toss olives and parsley together in another bowl.

2. Lay 4 tortillas on a flat surface and divide ½ of cheese over each. Spread about ½ cup olives over cheese, then sprinkle remaining cheese on top.

3. Slide 1 covered tortilla into a 10-inch skillet over medium heat. Place 1 of the remaining tortillas on top. Press down with a wide spatula to remove any air pockets. Cover and cook 1–2 minutes, checking frequently, until bottom tortilla is crisp and browned.

4. Turn over, cover, and cook 1–2 minutes more, or until lightly browned. Repeat this process for remaining quesadillas. Cut into wedges and serve immediately.

DESSERTS

CHERRY
CRISP

MAKES 4 TO 6 SERVINGS

With the tart cherries and the crispy coconut streusel, these are delightfully different dessert quesadillas.

8 (9- to 10-inch) white flour tortillas

16 ounces cream cheese, softened

1 teaspoon almond extract

½ teaspoon ground cinnamon

2 (18-ounce) cans cherry pie filling

Coconut Streusel (page 125)

1. Preheat oven to 400 degrees. Place a wire rack on a baking sheet.

2. Lay tortillas on a flat surface and spread cream cheese over each. Mix together almond extract, cinnamon, and pie filling in a bowl. Spread 1 cup cherry mixture over 4 tortillas.

3. Place 1 of the remaining tortillas on top of each covered tortilla, cream cheese side down. Press down with a wide spatula to remove any air pockets. Brush tops of tortillas with a little water. Spread ½ cup Coconut Streusel on top and press down with spatula, making sure streusel is pressed into tortilla.

4. Place quesadillas, streusel side up, on prepared baking sheet. It is okay if they overlap, but you may need to bake in batches. Bake 10–12 minutes, checking frequently so as not to burn. Cut into wedges and serve immediately.

PEACHES
AND CREAM

MAKES 4 TO 6 SERVINGS

The ginger makes the peaches pop with flavor and blends well with the almond-flavored cream cheese.

2 teaspoons almond extract

12 ounces light cream cheese, softened

8 (9- to 10-inch) white flour tortillas

4 cups (¼-inch slices) firm but ripe peeled peaches

2 tablespoons sugar

2 tablespoons butter

1 tablespoon grated fresh ginger

Few pinches ground nutmeg

Cinnamon sugar, to taste

Serving suggestions
Cinnamon Cream Syrup (page 126) or Vanilla Cream Syrup (page 123)

1. Mix almond extract with cream cheese in a bowl. Lay tortillas on a flat surface and spread cream cheese mixture over each.

2. Toss peaches in sugar in another bowl. In a large skillet, sauté peaches in butter, ginger, and nutmeg over medium-high heat, stirring constantly to brown but not burn. Spread about 1 cup peach mixture over 4 tortillas.

3. Slide 1 covered tortilla into a 10-inch skillet over medium heat. Place 1 of the remaining tortillas on top, cream cheese side down. Press down with a wide spatula to remove any air pockets. Cover and cook 1–2 minutes, checking frequently, until bottom tortilla is crisp and browned.

4. Turn over, cover, and cook 1–2 minutes more, or until lightly browned. Repeat this process for remaining quesadillas. Sprinkle with cinnamon sugar. Cut into wedges and serve immediately.

WALNUT-CRUSTED CRAN-APPLE

MAKES 4 TO 6 SERVINGS

Cranberries and apples make a sweet and tart filling for this luscious dessert.

1 teaspoon ground cinnamon

16 ounces light cream cheese, softened

8 (9- to 10-inch) white flour tortillas

4 cups (⅛-inch slices) Granny Smith apples

2 tablespoons butter

2 tablespoons brown sugar

1 cup dried sweetened cranberries

1 large egg mixed with 1 tablespoon water

1 cup minced or ground walnuts

Canola oil spray

Serving suggestions

Cinnamon Cream Syrup (page 126) or Rich Caramel Sauce (page 124)

1. Preheat oven to 400 degrees. Place a wire rack on a baking sheet.

2. Mix cinnamon with cream cheese in a bowl. Lay tortillas on a flat surface and spread cream cheese mixture over each.

3. In a large skillet, sauté apple slices in butter and brown sugar over medium-high heat for about 5 minutes, or until apple slices are soft and browned and liquid has evaporated. Spread 1 cup apple mixture over 4 tortillas. Sprinkle cranberries over apples.

4. Place 1 of the remaining tortillas on top of each covered tortilla, cream cheese side down. Press down with a wide spatula to remove any air pockets. Brush tops of quesadilla with a little egg wash. Spread ¼ cup walnuts on top and press down with spatula, making sure walnuts are pressed into tortilla. Spray with canola oil spray.

5. Place quesadillas, almond-crusted side up, on prepared baking sheet. It is okay if they overlap, but you may need to bake in batches. Bake 10–12 minutes, checking frequently so as not to burn. Cut into wedges and serve immediately.

CARAMEL APPLE

Caramel apple flavors in a crispy cinnamon-sugar tortilla crust make an easy and luscious dessert.

8 (9- to 10-inch) white flour tortillas

12 ounces light cream cheese, softened

4 cups (⅛-inch slices) Granny Smith apples

3 tablespoons butter

¼ cup brown sugar

Cinnamon sugar, to taste

Rich Caramel Sauce (page 124)

1. Lay tortillas on a flat surface and spread cream cheese over each.

2. In a large skillet, sauté apples, butter, and brown sugar over medium-high heat for about 5 minutes, or until apple slices are soft and browned and liquid has evaporated. Spread 1 cup apple mixture over 4 tortillas.

3. Slide 1 covered tortilla into a 10-inch skillet over medium heat. Place 1 of the remaining tortillas on top, cream cheese side down. Press down with a wide spatula to remove any air pockets. Cover and cook 1-2 minutes, checking frequently, until bottom tortilla is crisp and browned.

4. Turn over, cover, and cook 1-2 minutes more, or until lightly browned. Repeat this process for remaining quesadillas. Sprinkle with cinnamon sugar and drizzle with caramel sauce. Cut into wedges and serve immediately.

MANGO MADNESS

MAKES 4 TO 6 SERVINGS

Mango and pineapple make for a lively combination, and you'll love this unique almond crust!

1 teaspoon almond extract

1 (8-ounce) can crushed pineapple, drained

8 ounces light cream cheese, softened

8 (9- to 10-inch) white flour tortillas

1 large mango, peeled, pitted, and thinly sliced

1 egg, mixed with 1 tablespoon water

1 cup minced or ground almonds

2 tablespoons olive oil or olive oil spray

Serving suggestions
Cinnamon Cream Syrup (page 126) or Vanilla Cream Syrup (page 123)

1. Preheat oven to 400 degrees. Place a wire rack on a baking sheet.

2. Mix almond extract and pineapple with cream cheese in a bowl.

3. Lay tortillas on a flat surface and spread cream cheese mixture over each. Spread mango slices evenly over 4 tortillas, covering cream cheese mixture completely.

4. Place 1 of the remaining tortillas on top of each covered tortilla, cream cheese side down. Press down with a wide spatula to remove any air pockets. Brush tops of quesadillas with a little egg wash. Spread ¼ cup almonds on top and press down with spatula, making sure almonds are pressed into tortilla. Brush or spray olive oil on top.

5. Place quesadillas, almond-crusted side up, on prepared baking sheet. It is okay if they overlap, but you may need to bake in batches. Bake 10-12 minutes, checking frequently so as not to burn. Cut into wedges and serve immediately.

TRIPLE CHOCOLATE DECADENCE

MAKES 4 TO 6 SERVINGS

Chocolate, chocolate, and more chocolate—
decadence stuffed into a quesadilla!

8 ounces light cream cheese, softened

½ cup chocolate-hazelnut spread

8 (9- to 10-inch) white flour tortillas

8 ounces dark chocolate, broken into small pieces

12 ounces semisweet chocolate chips

Fresh raspberries, for garnish (optional)

Serving suggestion
Chocolate Decadence Sauce (page 125)

1. Mix cream cheese and chocolate-hazelnut spread in a bowl. Lay tortillas on a flat surface and spread cream cheese mixture over each. Sprinkle dark chocolate pieces over 4 tortillas.

2. Slide 1 covered tortilla into a 10-inch skillet over medium heat. Place 1 of the remaining tortillas on top, cream cheese side down. Press down with a wide spatula to remove any air pockets. Cover and cook 1–2 minutes, checking frequently, until bottom tortilla is crisp and browned.

3. Turn over, cover, and cook 1–2 minutes more, or until lightly browned. Repeat this process for remaining quesadillas. Sprinkle with chocolate chips and let sit for 1–2 minutes, or until melted. Spread melted chocolate chips over tortilla and garnish with raspberries if desired. Cut into wedges and serve immediately.

FOUR-LAYER FOLDED CHOCOLATE-HAZELNUT AND STRAWBERRY

MAKES 4 SERVINGS

Layers of strawberries and bananas with chocolate-hazelnut spread—a heavenly dessert ready in just minutes!

1 cup diced fresh strawberries

2 tablespoons strawberry jam

4 (8- to 10-inch) white flour tortillas

4 tablespoons chocolate-hazelnut spread

2 bananas, mashed with a fork

4 tablespoons cream cheese, softened

1. Mix strawberries with jam in a small bowl.

2. Place 1 tortilla on a cutting board, and with tip of a knife at center of tortilla, cut from center out to edge of tortilla.

3. On first quarter of tortilla, next to cut, spread ¼ of strawberry mixture. On second quarter of tortilla, spread 1 tablespoon chocolate-hazelnut spread. On third quarter, spread about 2 tablespoons mashed banana. On fourth quarter, spread 1 tablespoon cream cheese.

4. Beginning at cut edge, fold quarter with cream cheese up over quarter with banana, then fold again over quarter with chocolate-hazelnut spread, and finally fold over quarter with strawberries. You will have a 4-layer quesadilla in a wedge with bare tortilla on both top and bottom.

5. Heat a 10-inch skillet over medium-low heat and place folded quesadilla in skillet. Cover and cook about 2 minutes, watching closely until bottom side is golden brown. Turn over, cover, and cook another 2 minutes or so. Repeat this process to make 3 more quesadillas. Serve immediately.

BERRIES
AND BRIE

MAKES 4 TO 6 SERVINGS

The strong flavor of Brie is mellowed by the sweet berries,
making a creamy delight.

8 (9- to 10-inch)
white flour tortillas

8 ounces Brie, warmed

2 cups (⅛-inch slices)
fresh strawberries

1 cup fresh or thawed
frozen raspberries

1 cup fresh or thawed
frozen blueberries

2 tablespoons sugar

2 ounces Monterey
Jack cheese, shredded

Cinnamon sugar,
to taste

Serving suggestions
Fresh Fruit Purée
(page 124) or
Honey-Lime Fruit
Salsa (page 126)

1. Lay tortillas on a flat surface and spread Brie over each.

2. Toss berries with sugar in a bowl. Spread 1 cup berry mixture over 4 tortillas, then sprinkle with Monterey Jack cheese.

3. Slide 1 covered tortilla into a 10-inch skillet over medium heat. Place 1 of the remaining tortillas on top, Brie side down. Press down with a wide spatula to remove any air pockets. Cover and cook 1–2 minutes, checking frequently, until bottom tortilla is crisp and browned.

4. Turn over, cover, and cook 1–2 minutes more, or until lightly browned. Repeat this process for remaining quesadillas. Sprinkle with cinnamon sugar as desired. Cut into wedges and serve immediately.

FOUR-LAYER FOLDED
BANANA SPLIT

MAKES 4 SERVINGS

The classic '50s ice cream shoppe dessert is delicious folded into a quesadilla.

4 (9- to 10-inch) white flour tortillas

4 tablespoons cream cheese, softened

¼ cup chocolate-hazelnut spread

2 bananas, peeled and cut into ¼-inch slices

1 (15-ounce) can crushed pineapple, well drained

½ cup toasted almonds, chopped

1 (12-ounce) jar maraschino cherries, drained and chopped

1. Lay tortillas on a flat surface and spread cream cheese over each.

2. Place 1 tortilla on a cutting board, and with tip of a knife at center of tortilla, cut from center out to edge of tortilla.

3. On first quarter of tortilla, next to cut, spread ¼ of chocolate-hazelnut spread. On second quarter of tortilla, lay on ¼ of banana slices. On third quarter, spread about 2 tablespoons pineapple. On fourth quarter, scatter ¼ of almonds and cherries.

4. Beginning at cut edge, fold quarter with chocolate-hazelnut spread up over quarter with banana, then fold again over quarter with pineapple, and finally fold over quarter with almonds and cherries. You will have a 4-layer quesadilla in a wedge with bare tortilla on both top and bottom.

5. Heat a 10-inch skillet over medium-low heat and place folded quesadilla in skillet. Cover and cook about 2 minutes, watching closely until bottom side is golden brown. Turn over, cover, and cook another 2 minutes or so. Repeat this process to make 3 more quesadillas. Serve immediately.

PEANUT BUTTER AND APPLE

MAKES 4 TO 6 SERVINGS

This combination makes a delicious and easy after-school snack.

⅔ cup peanut butter

3 tablespoons honey

8 ounces light cream cheese, softened

8 (9- to 10-inch) white flour tortillas

2 peeled and cored large Golden Delicious apples, grated or chopped

Cinnamon sugar, to taste

Serving suggestions
Cinnamon Cream Syrup (page 126) or Rich Caramel Sauce (page 124)

1. Mix peanut butter and honey with cream cheese in a bowl. Lay tortillas on a flat surface and spread cream cheese mixture over each. Spread ½ cup apples over cream cheese mixture on 4 tortillas.

2. Place 1 covered tortilla in 10-inch skillet over medium heat. Place 1 of the remaining tortillas on top, cream cheese side down. Press down with a wide spatula to remove any air pockets. Cover and cook 1-2 minutes, checking frequently, until bottom tortilla is crisp and browned.

3. Turn over, cover, and cook 1-2 minutes more, or until lightly browned. Repeat this process for remaining quesadillas. Sprinkle generously with cinnamon sugar. Cut into wedges and serve immediately.

S'MORES

MAKES 4 TO 6 SERVINGS

**This twist on the gooey campfire favorite is
sure to have you licking your fingers!**

8 (9- to 10-inch)
white flour tortillas

8 ounces light cream
cheese, softened

2 cups mini
marshmallows,
plus more for
optional garnish

4 (1.5-ounce) bars
milk chocolate

4 tablespoons
butter, melted

½ cup graham
cracker crumbs

2 tablespoons sugar

Canola oil spray

1. Preheat oven to 400 degrees. Place a wire rack on a baking sheet.

2. Lay tortillas on a flat surface and spread cream cheese over each. Sprinkle ½ cup marshmallows over 4 tortillas. Crumble chocolate bars and sprinkle evenly over marshmallows.

3. Place 1 of the remaining tortillas on top of each covered tortilla, cream cheese side down. Press down with a wide spatula to remove any air pockets. Brush tops of quesadillas with a little butter. Mix together graham cracker crumbs and sugar. Spread graham cracker mixture on top of quesadillas and press down with spatula, making sure mixture is pressed into tortillas. Spray with canola oil spray.

4. Place quesadillas, graham cracker–crusted side up, on prepared baking sheet. It is okay if they overlap, but you may need to bake in batches. Bake 10–12 minutes, checking frequently so as not to burn. Garnish with additional marshmallows, if desired. Cut into wedges and serve immediately.

PECAN-CRUSTED PEAR

MAKES 4 TO 6 SERVINGS

Silky pears with crunchy pecans are a flavorful match.

2 tablespoons orange marmalade or other tart jam or jelly

12 ounces light cream cheese, softened

8 (9- to 10-inch) white flour tortillas

4 cups (⅛-inch slices) Bartlett pears

1 large egg mixed with 1 tablespoon water

1 cup minced or ground pecans

2 tablespoons olive oil or olive oil spray

Serving suggestions
Cinnamon Cream Syrup (page 126) or Vanilla Cream Syrup (page 123)

1. Preheat oven to 400 degrees. Place a wire rack on a baking sheet.

2. Mix marmalade with cream cheese in a bowl. Lay tortillas on a flat surface and spread cream cheese mixture over each. Spread pear slices evenly over 4 tortillas.

3. Place 1 of the remaining tortillas on top of each covered tortilla, cream cheese side down. Press down with a wide spatula to remove any air pockets. Brush tops of quesadillas with a little egg wash. Spread ¼ cup pecans on top and press down with spatula, making sure pecans are pressed into tortilla. Brush or spray olive oil on top.

4. Place quesadillas, pecan-crusted side up, on prepared baking sheet. It is okay if they overlap, but you may need to bake in batches. Bake 10–12 minutes, checking frequently so as not to burn. Cut into wedges and serve immediately.

SALSAS AND SAUCES

SASSY SMOKY SALSA

MAKES ABOUT 6 CUPS

1 lime, juiced (about 2 tablespoons)

2 cloves garlic, peeled

1 small bunch cilantro

About 6 large ripe tomatoes (to make 4 cups smashed)

2 teaspoons chipotle chile powder

1 teaspoon salt, or more to taste

1 tablespoon olive oil

2 to 3 Anaheim or jalapeño peppers, or a combination, seeded and minced

1 bell pepper, any color, seeded and minced

1 bunch green onions, with tops, sliced

A little sugar, if needed

1 (6-ounce) can tomato paste, if needed

Combine lime juice, garlic, and cilantro in a food processor and blend until smooth. Transfer to a large bowl. Cut tomatoes into quarters and squeeze out excess liquid. Mash with a potato masher until just chopped and add to bowl. Add chile powder, salt, olive oil, Anaheim peppers, bell pepper, and green onions. Stir all ingredients together and let sit on counter for at least 1 hour for flavors to blend. Taste and, if necessary, add a little sugar. If salsa is too runny, stir in tomato paste as needed. Cover and refrigerate up to 10 days.
Serve at room temperature.

ROASTED RED PEPPER
SAUCE

MAKES ABOUT 3 CUPS

3 red bell peppers, seeded

Canola oil

1 (16-ounce) container sour cream

3 tablespoons tomato paste

1 tablespoon lemon juice

1 teaspoon salt

Preheat broiler with rack about 6 inches from heat source. Cut bell peppers into 1-inch flattened strips and place skin side up on a baking sheet. Brush with a little canola oil and broil for 3–5 minutes, or until skins are lightly browned. Place in a blender with remaining ingredients. Blend until smooth. Refrigerate until ready to use.

SOUR CREAM–PAPRIKA
SAUCE

MAKES ABOUT 1 CUP

1 cup light sour cream

2 tablespoons lime juice

1 tablespoon honey

2 teaspoons smoked paprika

1 teaspoon ground cumin

Whisk together all ingredients in a bowl. Refrigerate until ready to use.

SOUTHWEST PESTO SAUCE

MAKES ABOUT 1 CUP

2 cups chopped fresh cilantro

¼ cup chopped fresh mint or basil

½ cup pine nuts

3 cloves garlic, peeled

1 jalapeño pepper, seeded

1 tablespoon lime juice

1 tablespoon honey

½ teaspoon salt

½ cup extra virgin olive oil

In a food processor, blend cilantro, mint, pine nuts, garlic, jalapeño, lime juice, honey, and salt until smooth. Slowly pour in olive oil and combine. Store in a covered container in the refrigerator.

MUSHROOM CREAM SAUCE

MAKES 2 CUPS

2 cups thinly sliced cremini mushrooms

3 tablespoons minced garlic

1 tablespoon butter

½ cup chicken or vegetable broth

½ cup heavy cream

2 tablespoons white wine vinegar

1 teaspoon salt

In a skillet, sauté mushrooms and garlic in butter for 3–5 minutes, or until softened. Stir in broth, cream, vinegar, and salt and cook until reduced by half. Transfer to a blender and blend until smooth. Serve warm.

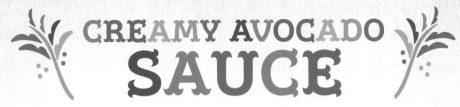

CREAMY AVOCADO SAUCE

MAKES ABOUT 2 CUPS

3 ripe avocados, peeled and pitted

3 cloves garlic, peeled

¼ cup mayonnaise

2 tablespoons lemon juice

1 teaspoon ground cumin

Salt and ground black pepper to taste

Process all ingredients in a food processor until smooth. Refrigerate until ready to use.

SPICY MUSTARD SAUCE

MAKES ABOUT 1 ½ CUPS

1 cup mayonnaise

¼ cup light sour cream

¼ cup spicy brown mustard

1 tablespoon grated horseradish

Salt and ground black pepper, to taste

Combine all ingredients in a bowl. Refrigerate until ready to use.

MOJO MARINADE

MAKES ABOUT 1 ½ CUPS

1 cup pineapple juice

1 lime, zested and juiced

1 orange, zested and juiced

1 canned chipotle chile pepper in adobo sauce, minced

1 ½ teaspoons cumin

2 tablespoons chopped fresh oregano leaves

2 teaspoons salt

Mix together all ingredients in a bowl and use as directed.

WHITE CHEDDAR SAUCE

MAKES ABOUT 3 CUPS

3 tablespoons butter

2 tablespoons flour

2 cups milk

4 ounces sharp white cheddar cheese, shredded

1 ounce Parmesan cheese, grated

Ground nutmeg, salt, and ground black pepper to taste

Melt butter in a skillet over medium-high heat. Stir in flour until absorbed. Whisk in milk. Slowly stir in cheeses. Simmer until thickened slightly. Add a few pinches of nutmeg, salt, and pepper. Serve warm.

PEACH CHUTNEY

MAKES ABOUT 2 CUPS

3 peaches, peeled, pitted, and diced

8 ounces low-sugar peach or apricot preserves

2 tablespoons rice vinegar

1 tablespoon minced fresh ginger

2 green onions, thinly sliced

1 teaspoon salt

In a saucepan, simmer together all ingredients for 5–8 minutes over medium-high heat, or until thickened. Serve warm or at room temperature.

VANILLA CREAM SYRUP

MAKES ABOUT 2 CUPS

1 cup heavy cream

½ cup sugar

1 tablespoon flour

4 large egg yolks

1 tablespoon vanilla

1 cup vanilla ice cream

In a saucepan, bring cream and sugar to a boil over medium-high heat. In a small bowl, mix together flour, egg yolks, and vanilla. Add a few spoonfuls boiling cream mixture, then add egg yolk mixture to cream mixture and stir constantly for 3 minutes. Add ice cream and continue to cook another 3 minutes, stirring constantly until thickened. Serve warm.

RICH CARAMEL SAUCE

MAKES ABOUT 2 CUPS

½ cup white sugar

½ cup brown sugar

½ cup heavy cream

4 tablespoons butter

½ teaspoon salt

1 teaspoon vanilla

In a saucepan, combine both sugars, cream, butter, and salt and bring to a boil over medium-high heat. Boil about 1 minute to soft-ball stage, or 230–240 degrees. Remove from heat and stir in vanilla. Cool to room temperature and serve.

FRESH FRUIT PURÉE

MAKES ABOUT 2 CUPS

3 cups fresh fruit or berries

2 tablespoons pure maple syrup

2 tablespoons light corn syrup

1 teaspoon lemon zest

1 tablespoon lemon juice

In a blender, blend all ingredients. Add water if necessary to reach desired syrup consistency. Refrigerate until ready to use.

COCONUT STREUSEL

MAKES ABOUT 3 CUPS

8 tablespoons butter

1 cup flour

1 cup brown sugar

½ cup rolled oats

½ cup sweetened coconut flakes

½ cup chopped walnuts

1 teaspoon ground cinnamon

1 teaspoon salt

In a bowl, mix together all ingredients with a pastry blender and use as directed.

CHOCOLATE DECADENCE SAUCE

MAKES ABOUT 2 CUPS

1 cup heavy cream

½ cup light corn syrup

½ teaspoon salt

8 ounces semisweet chocolate chips

In a saucepan, bring cream, corn syrup, and salt to a boil over medium-high heat. Remove from heat and add chocolate. Let stand about 5 minutes, until chocolate is melted, and then stir. Cool to room temperature and serve.

HONEY-LIME FRUIT SALSA

MAKES ABOUT 4 CUPS

4 cups diced fresh fruits, such as mango, strawberries, and kiwi

¼ cup honey

1 teaspoon lime zest

2 tablespoons lime juice

Mix together all ingredients in a bowl. Refrigerate until ready to use.

CINNAMON CREAM SYRUP

MAKES ABOUT 2 CUPS

1 cup sugar

½ cup corn syrup

½ teaspoon ground cinnamon

½ cup evaporated milk

In a small saucepan, combine sugar, corn syrup, and cinnamon. Bring to a boil over medium-high heat and stir for 3 minutes. Remove from heat and cool 5 minutes. Stir in evaporated milk. Serve warm.

INDEX

METRIC CONVERSION CHART

Volume Measurements		Weight Measurements		Temperature	
U.S.	**Metric**	**U.S.**	**Metric**	**Fahrenheit**	**Celsius**
1 teaspoon	5 ml	½ ounce	15 g	250	120
1 tablespoon	15 ml	1 ounce	30 g	300	150
¼ cup	60 ml	3 ounces	90 g	325	160
⅓ cup	75 ml	4 ounces	115 g	350	180
½ cup	125 ml	8 ounces	225 g	375	190
⅔ cup	150 ml	12 ounces	350 g	400	200
¾ cup	175 ml	1 pound	450 g	425	220
1 cup	250 ml	2¼ pounds	1 kg	450	230